Praise for True Stories...

Few stories have ever been told of the gallant, but often cruel and insensitive, experiences of "Blacks in Blue." In *True Stories of Over 100 Years* of combined service, three retired Black heads of a local Police Department and Sheriff's Office in the South describe their lives and how they made their mark as courageous "Blacks in Blue."

These men clearly exhibited the indomitable leadership, strength, and capabilities that produced excellence in the law enforcement system. Despite the racism, prejudice, and bigotry that was so common in southern cities and towns throughout the south, these awesome Black law enforcement leaders prevailed.

Police Chief Willie Johnson, Sheriff's Captain Calvin Kelley and Police Captain Willie Harper are the three remarkably exemplary Black leaders in blue who came from humble beginnings, yet they moved up the ladders of their majority White organizations.

The adversities of being Black did not impair their success in fairly enforcing the law, and elevating to the highest heights, within their majority White police and sheriff agencies. Moreover, they maintained strong and vibrant families at home, while being active in their churches and the community.

The advice and encouragement of these amazing "Blacks in Blue" make them great role models for all law enforcement officers in general, and for current and future "Blacks in Blue" in particular.

Honorable Leola Robinson-Simpson
SC House of Representatives (Dist. No 25)

True Stories of Over 100 Years...

Calvin Kelley, a longtime friend and associate, has written a down-to-earth, evocative, real-life story of a young Black man growing up in a family in Greenville, SC during the waning years of Jim Crow and rising to the highest level of local law enforcement in Greenville County. His book is a delight to read. He delivers a gripping account of what shaped his life and chosen career. Through it all, he demonstrates an unshakeable bond to his friends, family, and chosen profession. Calvin has rendered the whole of Greenville County a big service. His book is a must-read.

Johnny Mack Brown
Sheriff 1977-2001, Retired
U.S. Marshal for SC 2002-2010
Sheriff 2018-2020, Retired

True Stories of Over 100 Years...

After living in Greenville for the past 35 years, it is an honor to know that our community has been under the passionate and skilled leadership of Johnson, Kelley, and Harper. Upon reading the vocational history of these men, I am moved by their spirited fervor to withstand and overcome the challenges while staying focused on the job. Their biographical narratives give one a historical view of the cultural challenges that make Greenville, SC the city it has become. As you read the chapters, you are able to appreciate the character and integrity of these men as they sacrificed themselves for the sake of our community. These men, indeed, have all played a significant role in the development of Greenville as we now know it! I am honored to have served as a city police chaplain, colleague, and citizen of this community during the tenure of these men. They have represented well.

Dr. Toney C. Parks
Greenville City Police Chaplain,
Distinguished Professor of Practical Ministry
Erskine Theological Seminary,
Sr. Pastor Mt. Sinai Missionary Baptist Church
Greenville, SC

True Stories of Over 100 Years...

"Representation matters!" These words served as the impetus for Retired Chief Willie Johnson, Retired Captain Calvin Kelley, and Retired Captain Willie Harper to collectively serve over 100 years as Blacks in Blue.

From their unassuming beginnings, these valiant men endured racism and perilous trials, yet they persisted in their calling. In *True Stories...*, these gentlemen's meticulously crafted chronicles encompass their passion for the profession and pride in their military service. The book further bespeaks their selfless character, fidelity to community advancement, and staunch dedication to facilitating the way for future officers and leaders.

The personal and domestic lives of these men of valor are also central to the power of the book. All having been married to their middle or high school sweethearts for a combined 150 years, their marriages and family obligations upstage their career service, which is all too often an insurmountable feat, especially for those holding leadership positions.

The commonalities of these powerful men include their unbreakable bonds, which have contributed to their deep-rooted friendship and serve as the springboard for *True Stories...* This multiple-authored book offers readers glimpses into the daily experiences of the Blue, yet it casts an introspective, veracious light for those considering the profession. BEWARE!!! AUDACITY, TENACITY, and INTREPIDITY are compulsory!!!!!!!

Dr. Sonia Cunningham Leverette
Retired Assistant Superintendent in Education
Amazon Bestselling Author
Africanstore.net Bestselling Author

True Stories of Over 100 Years...

True Stories
of over
100 Years
from
Blacks in Blue

Written By

Retired Chief Willie Johnson,
Retired Captain Calvin Kelley and
Retired Captain Willie Harper

Hadassah's Crown Publishing, LLC

True Stories of Over 100 Years…

Copyright © 2022 by
Willie Johnson, Calvin Kelley, and Willie Harper

All rights reserved. No part of this book may be reproduced, scanned, or distributed in any printed or electronic form or by any means without prior written consent of the publisher, except for brief quotes used in reviews. Please do not participate in or encourage piracy of copyrighted materials in violation of the author's rights. Purchase only authorized editions.

Library of Congress Control Number: 2022903452
ISBN 978-1-950894-68-0

Published by Hadassah's Crown Publishing
634 NE Main St #1263
Simpsonville, SC 29681
HadassahsCrownPublishing.com

The publisher gratefully acknowledges permission
to reprint from *The Greenville News*.

Disclaimer: This book is memoir. It reflects the authors' present recollections of experiences over time. Some names and characteristics have been changed to protect the innocent and the guilty, and some events have been compressed.

Printed in the United States of America

True Stories of Over 100 Years…

Introduction

This book is written by three senior retired African American law enforcement officers with over 100 years of combined service. The three of us started our law enforcement careers in the early 1970's at the Greenville Police Department in Greenville, South Carolina within 36 months (Johnson in July of 1970, Kelley in August of 1970 and Harper in January of 1974). We began as patrolmen and worked our way up through the ranks. Johnson rose to the rank of police chief, and Harper and Kelley rose to the ranks of captain and/or senior commanders.

When we began as patrolmen, it was just a job, and we were just making a living. However, along the way, we made a difference within our departments.

These are our stories which are written to set the record straight from our perspectives. They are not to throw shade or shame.

Our stories!

True Stories of Over 100 Years…

Lady Justice
by Sirena Harris

True Stories of Over 100 Years…

Contents

In the Beginning   5
    Johnson   5
    Kelley   21
    Harper   35

Military & Early Career   49
    Johnson   49
    Kelley   87
    Harper   107

Highlights, Challenges, & Accomplishments   129
    Johnson   129
    Kelley   153
    Harper   161

Advice to Current & Future Officers   197
    Johnson   197
    Kelley   203
    Harper   209

If You See Something Say Something   213
    Johnson   213
    Harper   217

Photos and Memorabilia   223
    Johnson   223
    Kelley   237

Friends for Life   251
    Harper   251

Acknowledgments   257
    Kelley   257

Afterword   261

About the Authors   262

True Stories of Over 100 Years…

True Stories of Over 100 Years…

Retired Chief Willie Johnson

This book is dedicated to my beautiful wife of 48 years, Jannie Ferguson Johnson, along with my children, Shanoah, and Jamil, who have always supported and stood by me.

True Stories of Over 100 Years…

Chief Johnson
...in the Beginning

True Stories of Over 100 Years…

True Stories of Over 100 Years…

Though adversity met me twice during the first two weeks of my life, my family's response was the key factor and the foundation for my survival and success. Weighing only three pounds and losing my twin brother two weeks after birth caused my family to have great concerns. As a result, I was pampered and favored as a child. Born the youngest of four siblings in Laurens, South Carolina, I was blessed to have William and Ethel Davis Johnson as my parents.

Although I became the police chief in Greenville, SC, I came from very humble beginnings. In the rural area of Laurens County, the first ten years of my childhood were spent with my grandmother and family sharecropping on the farm. Sharecropping allows a tenant to farm on the land of a landlord in exchange for a share of the crop. I recall my siblings and cousins working in the field picking cotton, and although I accompanied them, I never had the tasks of the other children. We raised hogs, cows, and chickens, and a fond memory for me was having my first dog, Spot. I cherished the unconditional love that I received from Spot, a mixed-breed Beagle.

Knowing the importance of early literacy, my family made sure I received instruction. Furman Davis, my uncle, lived next door to my grandmother and visited our house three or four times a week to teach me to read. *The Three Little Pigs* and *Jack and Jill* were two of my favorite books. My uncle was determined I was going to read, and by the time I was four years old, I was reading those books and more. When I entered first grade, I was more advanced than my peers.

Tragedy struck in 1958 when my father died. My mother moved us from the farm to the suburbs of

True Stories of Over 100 Years…

Laurens County on Hookers Avenue. Her desire for our survival and well-being led my mother to work three jobs, and I cannot say enough about her selfless sacrifice.

While our new living experience was a major adjustment, one advantage was the new friends I met on our street. In the summertime, people came to our street looking for child labor. They sought youth to pick cotton or peaches, or cut grapes, so I chose to pick peaches for a man named Billy Patterson. I was a "box boy," which meant I placed the peaches in boxes. Working along with some other young boys, we loaded the boxes on a trailer, then to a semi-truck to be transported to a peach shed in Ora, S.C. It was an exciting and enjoyable job, since there were plenty of young girls picking peaches also. Talking to them was part of my daily motivation. The other motivator was our salary of five dollars a day, a generous amount of money at the time. I even worked on Saturdays and earned another two dollars and fifty cents.

Once when we were en route with a truckload of peaches taking them to the drop off location, we were involved in an accident. Two of us young boys were told to sit on top of the boxes to keep them balanced, putting us in danger. The careless driver, Mr. Pressley, drove extremely fast, causing the load to shift when we traveled around a curve. We had to jump up and run toward the front of the truck to prevent our falling off and into the street. If we had not done that, we would have been crushed under the falling boxes. Luckily, we were not injured and when we arrived, Billy Patterson was extremely upset with the truck driver.

My work ethic continued to reveal itself when I was young. I began picking wild blackberries during summers and selling them in White and Black neighborhoods for one dollar a gallon. One summer, I was employed by bricklayers, the Makins Brothers, tossing bricks up to them while they were on the scalpel laying them. Another year, the Laurens Hospital had a summer youth program, and I worked as an assistant to an orderly. This job was through a grant program, where the federal government reimbursed the hospital for hiring young people. Simpsons' Florist on East Main Street hired me to pull weeds out of the flower beds during another summer, and there must have been a million weeds in those beds! For four weeks during the summer, I worked. It was exhilarating to buy candy at Ben Franklin's Five & Dime Store, shop at

Rosenblum's or other stores on the square using my own money.

Looking back, growing up in Laurens was a challenge. However, it was invigorating and amusing at the same time because of the company I kept. I

(Fifth Grade Photo of Willie Johnson)

attended first through sixth grades at Sanders Elementary School, which was segregated. We used books that were passed down from the White school. We were separated and definitely not equal. I made more new friends there and had some splendid teachers as well. One teacher who stood out was Ms. Mary Whitener. She was very impactful on me because during story time, Mrs. Whitener read with such expression that it seemed each character came to life and jumped off the pages. The entire class anticipated story time, and everyone was present and engaged on those days.

From the age of thirteen to around fifteen or sixteen, I played Little League Baseball for Herbert Makins' team. I used to borrow a glove to play until I put one on layaway at Western Auto. Although it took two months for me to pay off a sixteen-dollar glove, I was determined to have my own. I paid two dollars down and went back every time I earned another two dollars from my summer work.

Beginning seventh grade at Sanders High School was fascinating as well. In the eighth grade, I joined the band. It cost thirty-five cents to attend a football game, and band members entered free. That was my motivation to join the band. I was a drummer and was amused to go around the house drumming on the furniture. Of course, my mother fussed about this. She would say, "Boy, if you do not stop beating on my table, I'm going to get a stick and beat you." Those times were the best. The experience of drumming proved useful later in my life.

True Stories of Over 100 Years...

A game-changer happened during my ninth-grade year. I took an agriculture class called Future Farmers of America, even though I never had any intention of becoming a farmer. Mr. Martin, my teacher, required us to participate in public speaking and learn parliamentary procedures. We studied parliamentary procedures in ninth through twelfth grades, and later in life, I realized that the class played a major part in my career, especially the public speaking aspect. When I was promoted to captain, the Black community, along with my wife Jannie, lavished me with a grand celebration. I was invited to speak at churches all over Greenville, Laurens, Pickens, and Columbia.

Desiring to pursue more macho activities during my junior and senior years in high school, I played football. Coach Jet Johnson had a very positive influence on me because he knew how to win. During my senior year, we won all of our football games except one. Coach Johnson was very aggressive, and once when we lost a game in the eleventh grade, he made us walk from the football field back to the high school as punishment. It was not a short distance. You can bet that made us not want to lose any more games. I lettered in football and received a purple and gold jacket with a big "S" that stood for Sanders. The girls loved to wear football players' jackets.

(Mrs. Jannie Ferguson Johnson)

True Stories of Over 100 Years…

There were not many opportunities for entertainment while I was in high school. One of the big events was a record hop at the Sanders gymnasium. Students who lived close enough to walk to the school attended. We paid twenty-five cents to enter, and once inside we segregated ourselves. All the boys went to one side of the gym and all of the girls went to the other.

Primarily during those dances, the boys liked to dance with the girls on the slow songs, and I remember "Rainbow 65" by Gene Chandler being one of my favorite songs to dance to. When the Temptations and the Four Tops' music hit the market, we purchased records for ninety-nine cents. I remember purchasing the Four Tops and playing one of their hits so often that my grandmother told me she was sick and tired of hearing that record. Other than buying records, we did not have much Black music we could listen to other than a DJ Randy on a station out of Nashville, Tennessee who came on from nine until two o'clock in the morning.

Another highlight from my high school years was patronizing Dr. Pughsley's Drug Store on the "Backstreet" (Black retail district) of Laurens to purchase a cheeseburger and a strawberry milkshake, then sit in the air-conditioned room to enjoy it. Air conditioning was not a luxury we enjoyed at home. We used fans and sat near the windows to cool off. Otherwise, we sat in the shade outside.

Watching movies at the Echo Theater was another favorite pastime when I was young. This was during segregation and the Colored kids sat upstairs while the White kids sat downstairs. Back in those days, Blacks were referred to as "Colored." It was somewhat degrading to us as the Colored kids to be viewed as less than the White kids. Inequality was certainly present, and Jim Crow Laws kept us separate.

During the fall of each year, my favorite memories were of attending the Laurens County Fair. Normally, I had two dollars to spend, and each ride costed about twenty cents. I rode twice with a girl and spent the rest on myself, buying cotton candy, candy apples, and hotdogs. When I reached the twelfth grade, I had saved twenty dollars for the fair. I thought I was rich, and that year's fair topped them all.

It occurred to me in high school and in my early teenage years that there wasn't a plethora of opportunities for Blacks in Laurens after graduation. When I was in twelfth grade, many boys started working in the mills. One of my friends shared with me that more workers were needed at Watts Mill, so I met with one of the supervisors. He proceeded to show me around the mill as well as the job I would perform. The supervisor introduced me to the plant workers, telling them that I was coming to work there. As he talked to them, he had to scream so they could hear him over the extremely loud machines. I was saying to myself, "Oh no. I do not want a job like this." That tour of the mill let me know I wanted nothing to do with a mill. It turned me off completely.

After graduating from high school, Voorhees College in Denmark, South Carolina topped my short list of schools. I took the SAT, submitted my application, and received an acceptance. I planned to attend at the end of August 1967. But during the summer, I heard that the Torrington Manufacturing Plant in Clinton, South Carolina was hiring. I went to Torrington with my friends, and we saw a supervisor from a construction company who was hired to replace the plant's roof. He hired the four of us, and we were thinking we were going to be working inside the plant. However, the job was replacing the building's roof. After climbing a ladder to the top of the building and seeing that the roof was made of tar and gravel, I realized that a pick and a shovel were needed to dig the old roof off before the new roof could be laid. We worked that day and did not bother to go back the next day. We were so done that we did not even stick around to get paid.

    When my friends and I returned to downtown Laurens, a recruiter was standing in front of the military recruitment office. He yelled for us to come over and talk to him, so we did. He asked if we were interested in joining the army. He showed us pictures of places we could visit and said that the army would pay for our education. I remembered when my mother told me I would be required to have a job while I attended Voorhees because she could not afford to pay for my education. I also remembered I did not like the job at Torrington, and I wanted nothing to do with mill life. Considering these factors, enlisting in the army was a good move.

True Stories of Over 100 Years…

Retired Captain Calvin Kelley

This book is dedicated to my beautiful wife,
Joaquina Kelley.

True Stories of Over 100 Years…

True Stories of Over 100 Years…

Captain Kelley
...in the beginning

True Stories of Over 100 Years…

True Stories of Over 100 Years…

In 1946, the first heavyweight title bout between the great Joe Louis and Billy Conn was broadcasted on television. Of course, Joe Louis won. On October 15 of that same year, I was born to Ruby Mae and Herbert Lee Kelley. I was their third of six children: three boys, and three girls. Growing up in the Southern Side Community of Greenville, South Carolina, near what was then called "The Southern Depot Train Station," I lived in a little "shotgun house" on Oscar Street. It was called a "shotgun house" because as you entered the front door, you could see clearly through to the back door, similar to the straightness of a shotgun barrel.

During the time I lived on Oscar Street, there were many rainfalls. You could hear the rain pounding like a thousand drums on the metal roof of our house. The rain was so heavy, my father stood watch in case our house started to flood. When the water levels reached a certain depth, my father packed my mother, my siblings, and me in our old car, and we headed up Washington Street to Roman Lane where my grandparents lived until the water began to recede. As we drove away, I remember looking back at what resembled a lake and chickens trying to escape the flood. I can still visualize when Civil Defense had to come in with boats to evacuate people from their homes.

Periodically, I travel back through the old community where I was born. There are reminders, like the home of Mrs. Mamie Norris, that still stands. Now sits a vacant lot where my family home once stood.

Back then, we did not have bathtubs in our homes, but we bathed in tin tubs. Once, our neighbors had prepared a hot bath for someone in their family. My younger sister, who was out playing, wandered over to their house and somehow ended up in that tin tub. She was scalded to the point that her skin just melted from her body. My father, as he always did, showed up just in time to wrap my sister in a sheet and transport her to the hospital. She remained there for a while, and she had skin grafted so her healing could begin. To this day, her scars remind us of that horrific event.

My father had to leave school at the age of eight and assume responsibility for his family after his father left home. At that time, my father, being the oldest of his two siblings, Thomas and Mae, had to assume the responsibility of a grown man and go to work.

There was a Syrian family, the Eassys, who owned a community grocery store on Hudson Street, and they gave my father a job. As years passed, my father won their confidence as a trustworthy employee and became a jack-of-all-trades in their businesses. The Eassys also owned a bottling company. My father ran the store, completed carpentry and plumbing work; you name it, he did it. Also, while working there, Father persuaded the owners to allow the community members to start accounts at the store where they could buy items on credit and pay them off at the end of the month. If it had not been for these newly established credit accounts, many people would have been unable to make ends meet financially. As a result of my father working for this family, some of my favorite childhood memories were of Christmas. When father came home on Christmas Eve, he brought big baskets of fruit, candy, and nuts from the Eassy family. Even though there were six of us, we always had a big Christmas.

Despite never receiving a formal education, Father was a wizard in math and had a business sense as if he were college educated. He was compassionate and very family-oriented. I wanted to do everything I could to make him proud. My father sacrificed to ensure that everyone's needs were met. To this day when certain situations arise, I ask myself, "how would Daddy handle this?" Growing up, my father was my idol. He was truly the epitome of what a real man and father should be.

My mother was referred to as "Queen" by her children because that is how we saw her. Along with being the caretaker for the home, she was also a nurse's aide at Greenville General Hospital for approximately thirty years. I have very fond memories of my mother, but the one I look back on now and laugh about is when she would tell on me for whatever devilment I had gotten into. As soon as my daddy entered the door, there were many days my mama said, "Calvin did...." Before I could get a word out, my daddy was saying, "This is gonna hurt me more than it's gonna hurt you."

My father's brother, Thomas Kelley, aka "Buster," worked for Textile Hall on Washington Street. Textile Hall during the time was like the Greenville Memorial Auditorium. If there was a concert or a function in town, it was held at Textile Hall. I remember annual ice-skating shows being a big deal back then. My uncle allowed my family and his family to enter into one of the back entrances and stand under the bleachers to watch. I'm not sure if we entered that way because we did not have tickets or because Blacks were not welcomed. I suspect the latter.

Our family moved from Oscar Street around 1952, and that move was unforgettable. The man who moved our belongings was a coal salesman. He drove a big truck that had a frame on the back that was leaning so badly, I thought it was going to fall over. It reminded me of Jed Clampett's truck from *The Beverly Hillbillies*. I can picture that man sweeping coal dust and fragments off the truck so we could load up our personal belongings. When he finally loaded the truck, I felt I was going to another country.

I was around six at that time and remember this as one of the most joyous times of my childhood. It was like I had died and gone to Heaven. We headed straight through town toward an area called Nicholtown to Fieldcrest Village, a brand-new community. It was so new that all of the roads were not yet paved. We were then able to take baths in a real bathtub with running, hot water.

When we walked into our new home, apartment 14A, I was overjoyed. We were the first family in the new apartment building. We now had six rooms! Six rooms! Our home was so spacious we could hear an echo when we talked. My family was thrilled for our new beginning.

After a few years passed, Reverend Jesse Jackson and his family moved into Fieldcrest Village. I could walk down our front stairs, take a right and enter the back of Reverend Jackson's house. His mother, Mrs. Helen Jackson, was den mother for my scout troop. As a kid, I retrieved the ball when Jesse used to practice kicking the ball in front of the house. Jesse and my oldest brother were classmates and teammates. They played basketball and baseball together at Sterling High School, and Jesse became a star football player for Sterling.

Attending school was never one of my favorite pastimes. I did not like reading, English, or math, and I definitely did not like homework. Back then, I thought I just needed to be able to count my money so I could make it in life. I never felt I had book smarts like my siblings. My oldest brother, Thomas, was great in sports, and my middle brother, Harold, was "as smart as a whip," as people used to say. My three sisters, Delores, Marion, and Deborah, were smart as well. I am the only person I know to ever receive an F in gym. Reason being, I did not like to sweat. Period!

However, what I did like to do was draw. In fact, I was known in high school for my drawings. During holidays like Christmas and Easter, teachers asked my friend James 'PeeWee' Jones and me to draw and paint pictures for their classes.

Another pleasure for me was taking pride in my appearance. I loved to dress. People used to say I was the sharpest person in the class. I loved clothes and always made sure I was neat and clean. My mother used to wash our jeans and use stretchers when she hung them out to dry. Then, she used Argo starch to crease our pants with an iron. We could hardly walk, but we were sharp!

While being educated at Sterling High School, I had to deal with some tough situations, including gangs. As an eleventh grader, there were boys from different areas feuding with each other. The guys were so bold they even jumped on teachers.

The boys from West Greenville and the boys from Nicholtown had a confrontation at one of the community centers over some young ladies. One afternoon while waiting on the bus, the boys from West Greenville surrounded me as I sat on a wall near the school. They hit me in the head with what felt like a baseball bat. The next thing I knew, my lights went out. Still to this day, I do not remember traveling home, but some young ladies helped me get on the bus. My mother and sisters waited for me to arrive home, since word had gotten to them that I had been jumped on. We were reluctant to call the police because we knew if the police were called for a Black-on-Black crime, nothing would become of it. The next school day, I was ready for revenge. I wasn't as concerned about the injuries I received; it was more about what happened in front of the girls standing at the bus stop with me. I was determined it would never happen again.

On the following Monday as I left school, I saw the boys who jumped me standing near "The Huddle," which was our local soda shop. As I walked toward them, one of the boys approached me and apologized. He said they thought I was someone else. Luckily, for them, I received an apology that day.

While I lived in Nicholtown, my friends and I gathered to talk on the corner on the weekends. I'd walk from my house and notice a familiar girl sitting on her back porch each time I passed. She knew my schedule down to the 'T' because she would be in that same spot on her porch every weekend at the same time. Her name was Joaquina, and one of the highlights of my high school career was meeting her. She was gorgeous! I knew of Joaquina while I lived in Fieldcrest Village, but we started dating when I was in the eleventh grade. We dated throughout my senior year, and after I graduated and joined the military, Joaquina and I continued our relationship through letters.

Sadly, Sterling High School burned down in 1967.

The cause was said to have been electrical issues, but the community felt otherwise. This was during the time in the South when schools were beginning to desegregate. It is believed that some Whites who were opposed to desegregation took it upon themselves to destroy our high school. The only thing that survived was the gym, and it is still there today. The Sterling Tiger pride will forever live on in each of us.

True Stories of Over 100 Years…

Retired Captain Willie Harper

This book is dedicated to my dear wife Winnie,
who I met 55 years ago.

True Stories of Over 100 Years…

True Stories of Over 100 Years…

Captain Harper
…in the Beginning

True Stories of Over 100 Years…

I was born in Laurens County, South Carolina, in an area called the "B. Bailey Place." When I was a year or so old, we moved to the City of Laurens, where we shared a three-room house on Chestnut Street with my grandmother. Our family grew to include a brother and sister. Our tin roof house did not have insulation; therefore, it was sweltering in the summers and cold in winters. The house did not include indoor plumbing. Our heat source was a wood heater, and we cooked on a black and white cast iron wood stove. We lived meagerly, but we were blessed and happy as a family.

When I was seven or eight, it became my responsibility to make sure we had kindling firewood during the winters. I was first up to start the fire on those bitterly cold mornings.

Our front yard was bare and covered with red clay where there should have been grass. If a sprig of grass or any greenery grew, we plucked it up. Brush brooms were all we needed to maintain our front yard, which often served as the playground for my brother, cousins, and me. Some of my cousins lived in the Projects, a community of brick buildings with gas heat and indoor plumbing. I often begged my mom to move to the Projects to no avail.

My mother made sure that church was an integral part of our lives. We often walked to Sunday School at Saint Paul Baptist Church on East Hampton Avenue, where some family members still worship.

My first day of school was an exciting time because I did not know what to expect. Public schools had not yet integrated, and the school system did not provide transportation for Black students. I have vivid memories of those days, such as separate water fountains and bathrooms in supposedly public spaces like the bus station. With distinctive signs that read

"Colored" and "White," unlike a male and female bathroom for Whites, there was only one bathroom for Blacks. Doctor offices were no different. They had separate waiting rooms, and Black patients had to wait until all the White patients were seen. I distinctly remember not being able to sit and wait like White people inside Eaddy Blake's Drugstore while a prescription was being filled.

My family did not own a vehicle and buses were not provided, so I walked to school my first year. I remember the school as an old wooden building shaped like an army barrack. It was one long building,

(Second Grade School Picture)

and the overall condition was terrible compared to today's standards. Mrs. Dial, my first-grade teacher, was demanding, but she made learning fun! Corporal punishment was standard; therefore, Mrs. Dial and other teachers administered physical punishment to students who failed to complete their schoolwork and for any minor disobedience. The following year, I attended a newly constructed school, Thomas Sanders Elementary, as a second grader. My mother decided the walk from home was too far, so she arranged a taxicab service as my mode of transportation to and from school. I didn't particularly like that school because the principal who had one arm always carried a wide strap, like barbers used to sharpen their straight razors. It seemed he was always waiting on an opportunity to use the strap on any student for any minor infraction. Yes, even for arriving late to school. It didn't matter why you were late. I was afraid of him.

    Despite my fear, I was a good student. I excelled in spelling. My first spelling bee came down to me and one other participant in the third grade, just the two of us left standing. I missed becoming the overall winner because of the word I was asked to spell; I spelled the word "disappointment" with two s's instead of one.

Because of my ability in spelling, my third through sixth-grade teachers often chose me to participate in spelling bees.

In fourth grade, Mr. Brunson was my 4H Club and agriculture teacher. Although I did not grow up in a rural area, agriculture became one of my favorite classes. Mr. Brunson assigned each student a class project. We were to start a small business and sell a service or product. Most students who lived on farms or rural areas grew and sold vegetables. With no farming experience and living in town, I had to be a bit creative. Because fishers often traveled Chestnut Street en route to Lake Greenwood, I chose to sell fishing worms. After removing the side panel from a discarded white refrigerator and writing "red worms for sale" on it, I nailed it to a big oak tree in our front yard. That assignment proved to be a profitable hustle that I continued until my junior year in high school. It was the beginning of a business mindset. Since then, I've always involved myself in some small business venture.

Reflecting on my elementary school years, I was probably called a teacher's pet. Mrs. Higgins, my fifth-grade teacher, often called upon me to write on the board for her. She also left me in charge of the class if she had to leave the classroom. Mrs. Mary Whitener, my sixth-grade teacher, also took an interest in me. As the librarian for the Black library in Laurens, she named me her library assistant. I have often wondered but never learned why she chose me as her library assistant. Each day after school, I rode with her to open the library. She taught me the book circulation process, but she always allowed enough time for me to read and study. The pay was not bad for a sixth grader. I was paid a fifty-cent piece each time I worked after school at the library.

My father lived in Washington, DC. I think I was nine or ten years old when I first traveled by train to visit him—leaving Laurens around 11:00 PM created within me both emotions of excitement and fear. The twelve-hour ride had many stops, but I didn't have to worry about finding or purchasing food since my mother prepared a meal for me and lovingly placed it in a shoebox. Her kindness served dual roles of creating warmth to relieve my loneliness and provision for my hunger. Much of my entertainment, which kept me awake, came from my window view as the train traveled over tall bridges and dark tunnels. One can easily imagine how I must have felt.

When the train pulled into the Washington, DC station, the tall buildings and masses of people all in one place at one time expanded my previously small, sheltered world. My father picked me up, and on the drive to his house, he pointed out several historical sites he thought were important. His mother lived in Philadelphia, so he drove us there for visits. That would be my first visit with my paternal grandmother. My father's three younger brothers lived with her. However, the oldest was serving in the Marine Corp. The younger two didn't hesitate and were eager to show their young country nephew around. It was exciting to ride bikes downtown via Walnut and Chestnut Streets. I formed a love for Philadelphia and for my grandmother's community, where I developed fond memories. While my father planned for me to stay with my grandmother for a couple of weeks, I stayed most of the summer. I fell in love with city life. There was inside plumbing, no firewood to cut, and kids all over the place.

In most cases, many people shape one's life; however, my mother was the most influential person in my life. She was an extraordinarily strong woman and a staunch disciplinarian. She preached integrity, and with the help of my grandmother, she raised three strong children. Loving memories of special times with her will forever remain with me. As a domestic worker, she walked to and from work, regardless of the weather. When it was near time for her to return home, my brother, sister, and I started looking up the street in the direction from which she would come. The minute we caught a glimpse of her, we'd take off running to meet her. Often, she would have some treat for us, usually candy.

Like most young kids, I was attracted to flashing lights, police, and military uniforms. The red and blue lights, whistling sirens, and the rapidly passing police and highway patrol cars on my street invigorated me. There was one friendly highway patrolman in particular who drove past my house daily. As we played in our front yard, he would slow down to speak or give my cousins and me a nice gesture. That was unusual because most police officers wouldn't speak to Black kids. When we finally got a thirteen-inch tv, there was one police show I always wanted to see. That show was "*M Squad*," about a Chicago detective named Frank Ballenger. Actor Lee Marvin played Ballenger, and that show caused me to dream of working as a Chicago police officer. I rarely saw a Black police officer while growing up in South Carolina. However, the many Black policemen in Washington, DC, and Philadelphia gave me hope. It inspired and instilled in me that a career in law enforcement was attainable.

When I graduated to seventh grade, I attended Sanders High School, a school for seventh through twelfth graders. There was no middle school in Laurens for Black students. My first couple of years at Sanders were uneventful. However, when I reached ninth or tenth grade, I started skipping classes, and my good friend, Gettis, aka "Meatball," introduced me to the pool room. I immediately developed an affinity for the game, and I still enjoy playing today. During high school, against my mother's directions, every opportunity I had, I played pool.

During segregation in the sixties, "Backstreet," now known as South Harper Street, had Black businesses such as cafes, clubs, barbershops, and the only Black movie theatre. Later on, the only Black drugstore, Pughsley's Pharmacy, opened, doubling as a food and soda bar. To this day, I have not savored a more delicious cheeseburger and ice cream soda than at that drug store. Pughsley's was the place to be in the heat of summers because it was the only air-conditioned spot on Backstreet. The Harlem Theatre was owned and operated by Mr. and Mrs. Robert Higgins (my fifth-grade teacher and her husband). The pool room opened around eight o'clock on Saturdays, and I was unashamed to await the door's opening. Backstreet was not the place for a teenager; I witnessed some terrible activities there. The local jailhouse was nearby, and I heard prisoners yelling out from being beaten and abused by law enforcement. From my Backstreet experience and living in Laurens, I observed activity by Laurens police officers and the state highway patrol that would not be tolerated today.

In tenth grade, I tried out for the football team. However, I didn't give myself much chance to make the team. Daily after practice, the coaches admonished us to go straight home and stay away from the joints where teens hung out. Most times, I did just the opposite. After practice, the coaches stopped by the pool room and other teenager hangouts; I was caught in the pool room too many times. As a result, I was told not to return to practice again in a very unkind way.

During my junior year in high school, I cleaned new

cars as they arrived at an auto dealership after school several days a week and on Saturday mornings. As a senior in high school, I earned $1.25 an hour working full-time on the second shift at the Laurens Mill. Before that, during my adolescent years, I worked odd jobs, such as cutting grass, raking leaves, and shoveling snow. I also sold the *Laurens Advertiser*, a weekly newspaper, where I earned three cents per paper out of the ten cents cost. I took drive-in orders mostly while working at a beer joint called "Specs." The owner and his wife also owned a more sophisticated drive-in restaurant called "The Hub," where I later worked. I spent most of my spare time in the pool room when I wasn't working. I developed a close relationship with the aging owner of the pool room on Backstreet. He not only taught me about the game of pool, but he also graciously shared his years of wisdom with me, mostly about life.

While working in the mill, I often considered a career in the military. The passing of my maternal grandmother a few weeks after my graduation prompted my decision to enlist in the army. If I did not volunteer, it was inevitable that I would serve because of the military draft. My graduation from high school was in June. In July, I enlisted in the army and reported for basic training at Fort Jackson, South Carolina.

True Stories of Over 100 Years…

Chief Johnson
Military & Early Career

True Stories of Over 100 Years…

True Stories of Over 100 Years...

After serving in the military for two or three weeks, I wondered what in the world I had done. The military is an institution that breaks you down and reshapes you to be the person they desire you to be. First, they cut off all my hair and provided me with ill-fitting clothes. My superiors told me when to go to bed and when to rise, and they expected me to run every time I stepped outside of the barracks. The running, they said, was to keep us motivated. I thought at the time it was too much!

Later, I appreciated that the army was helping me to grow into adulthood. I did not recognize it at the time, but after basic training, I realized the positive and impactful changes that strengthened my foundation as a leader with a strong work ethic.

One night, I heard a young man crying because he was drafted and did not want to be in the army. Someone reported this to the drill sergeant the next day and he verbally abused the young man, calling him

(Private E-1 Willie Johnson)

a 'mama's boy' and berating him in front of everyone. I knew I had to be strong! The sergeant suggested that we give the mama's boy a "blanket party," a term used to indicate a blanket being thrown over a soldier's head. Everyone was instructed to hit or punch the soldier, and the blanket prevented him from knowing who was responsible for the blows.

Once I was assigned "KP," kitchen patrol, where I scrubbed all of the dinner pots and pans. Some of the pots were large enough for me to stand in and they had to be scrubbed spotless. Needless to say, KP was not my duty of choice!

When the sergeant came around inquiring if anyone knew how to play drums, I did not immediately volunteer. I had heard you did not want to volunteer for anything in the army. But when the sergeant added that if you played drums you'd never have KP duty again, I volunteered. Playing drums was a challenge in itself, especially having to run everywhere we went. If the drill sergeant said, "Double time," I had to do double time while drumming. While this was challenging, it was not nearly as challenging as KP duty. Learning to play drums while in high school paid off for me in the army.

Drilling ceremonies are designed to teach soldiers how to march, preparing them for combat by rapidly carrying out orders and commands. This was where I had another advantage from my high school band days. When the drill sergeants noticed I knew the drill calls, they named me a squad leader during my second phase of training in the military.

When I finished basic training, I went to AIT, "Advanced Infantry Training," which was for combat duty. From that training, I was selected to attend NCO, "Non-Commissioned Officer Training," where I was trained to be a squad leader in Vietnam. At that time, the Vietnam War had begun. In Fort Benning, Georgia, I learned leadership and survival skills for twenty-two weeks. The blue patch on my shoulder read 'Follow Me,' the motto for the organization. I received more training in public speaking, but this time with a commanding voice. I was grateful for another exposure I had in high school. I received first aid, firearms training, and everything else required to equip me for a wartime situation. When I finished that training, I was promoted from Private E2 to Staff Sergeant E6. I graduated as the top candidate in my class on March 14, 1968. After graduation, I returned to Fort Jackson in Columbia, SC. I was in the Non-Commission Class Number 14-68, completing training on May 21, 1968. My two most important takeaways from the military were stay focused on your mission and the welfare of your people.

True Stories of Over 100 Years...

(Infantry Training Logo)

True Stories of Over 100 Years…

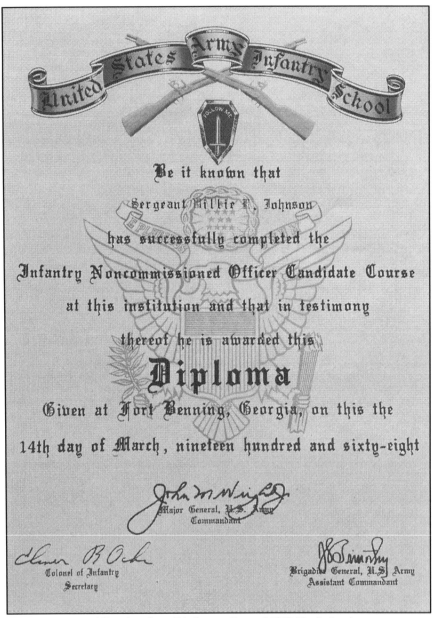

(Graduation Diploma from NCO Training)

In just eleven months, I was promoted from an E1 to an E6 in the Army. This was virtually unheard of, but I enlisted during a time when the military was preparing soldiers for the Vietnam War. The writing, speaking, and listening skills I gained in high school were beneficial in quickly propelling my advancement. In life, timing is everything, and it was on my side because I came along at the right time.

Beginning at the age of nineteen, I served in Vietnam for eighteen months. I recall a time when I was flown by helicopter to the jungles of Vietnam, thinking again, what had I done? There I was, a platoon sergeant assigned to lead thirty plus eighteen, nineteen, and twenty-year-old guys in a war zone. I found out quickly in situations like that, you fall back on your training. The infantry training was critical to my survival.

Somewhere around my seventh month in Vietnam, I acquired a case of malaria, which comes from mosquito bites. We were out in the jungle at the time, and I started running a high fever, causing my vision to blur. The platoon medic examined me and advised the company commander to send me to the hospital. The commander called in a "dust off" (a medical helicopter) and I was flown to a hospital in Chu Lai Vietnam. Lying on a stretcher, I heard the doctor say, "We're losing him." The medical staff cut off all of my clothes and put me on a metal bed with holes in the bottom. Then they covered me in ice, so much that my teeth chattered. Having an out-of-body experience as I looked down at the medic working on me, I could not speak. Today, the blood bank is very cautious in allowing me to donate because of my medical history with malaria.

The malaria experience was just one of the many life-changing moments for me during the Vietnam War. One of the soldiers in my platoon named Oakie loved to lead the patrols. He always said, "Sergeant, I will walk point if nobody else will." Oakie was a young White male from Georgia who had lied about his age and joined the army when he was only seventeen years old. One night when Oakie was on ambush patrol, the Viet Cong (enemy) crawled up close to his position and threw a grenade on him. He was killed and placed in a body bag. The image of his mangled body parts was forever etched in my mind. I'll never forget Oakie. His death made me very bitter toward the enemy. This was the first time I saw a deceased young soldier, and it had a negative effect on me. It caused me to have nightmares, even until this day. We were young, so I wanted to serve and return home safely. In the army, we had a saying, "I want to go back to the world." America was the world to us, and in Vietnam, there was nothing beneficial for us.

Most of the people we encountered in Vietnam lived in "hooches," which were dirt floor, straw roof dwellings held up by four poles. Those were their homes, and they were happy. We thought about how we were reared and how we complained about what we had in America. Compared to the Vietnamese, we were wealthy.

Despite the unsightly or unpleasant memories, comradery was a distinguished attribute for me as a soldier in Vietnam. Members of my platoon and I looked out for each other, and we were like brothers when we were in the jungles. If someone was out of water and needed a drink, we shared canteens without even wiping them off. We were that close. Once we were removed from those live-or-die situations, everything returned to normal. Blacks and Whites were segregated. In deadly situations, you bond with others for survival.

After serving in Vietnam for eight months, I was allowed to return home on a thirty-day leave. Thirty days later, I returned to Vietnam for another ten months. While back in Vietnam, I was shot at but thankfully I was not hit. I witnessed some terrible scenes, including many dead bodies, and incidents that young men normally aren't exposed to. There is no eloquent way to express the description that war is absolutely hell! One of the strangest experiences is hearing gunfire whizzing over your head, along with artillery going over you before it hits its target. Also, let me point out one of the happiest times you have is during mail call.

It was during my time in Vietnam that the American artist Freda Payne released her hit single, "Bring the Boys Home." This song was so powerful in provoking nostalgic emotions for soldiers that the military banned it from being played in Vietnam.

During my tour, I earned a week of R&R, (rest and recuperation), where I could leave Vietnam and go to another country. I chose Hong Kong, and that was an awakening! I met an approximately sixteen-year-old young lady whose father owned a camera booth on the street, primarily selling cameras to visiting soldiers. Her father asked my friend and me if we liked his daughter. He wanted one of us to marry her so she could return to the United States with us. Then maybe the family could also visit America. Some of the soldiers did exactly this. The girls usually stayed with the soldiers for a year, and then they moved to a Hong Kong community in the United States.

New police chief learned leadership in Vietnam

Greenville's 23rd chief is first to hold college degree, first African-American

By April E. Moorefield
STAFF WRITER
amoorefi@greenvillenews.com

Ask Greenville Police Chief Willie Johnson where he learned his most profound lessons about leadership and people, and he doesn't even pause to think.

It was in Vietnam.

A youngster who'd grown up in rural Laurens County, Johnson at 19 found himself submerged in what would eventually become a conflict that would throw the country into national protests and force the president not to seek re-election.

"It was there I learned how to be committed," Johnson said, reflecting on the path he took to become the city's 23rd police chief. "I learned to first be committed to the mission. And second, to the people who serve under your command."

Johnson took the reins of the Greenville Police Department in late July, succeeding former Chief Mike Bridges, who retired after more than a decade at the agency's helm. He spent 30 years working his way through the ranks from patrolman to major before being named the city's first black chief.

"It was a great honor that humbled me as a person," Johnson said of his unanimous selection by the Greenville City Council. "It showed me that you can make it in Greenville, South Carolina, and in America if you are a persistent and high-performance person who stays focused on your task."

Johnson, 51, was raised by his mother and grandmother in Laurens County's Ora community. Growing up, he toyed with the idea of becoming a schoolteacher. But after graduating from Sanders High School in 1967, he opted to join the Army.

In the military, he excelled and was chosen among his peers to attend special leadership and advanced training schools.

"But there was a catch," Johnson remembers. "Once the training was behind us, they shipped us out to Vietnam."

He received the Bronze Star, a Combat Air Medal and a Good Conduct Medal before returning to his na-

See CHIEF *on page 78*

In charge: Chief Willie Johnson sits in his office shortly after being named Greenville's new police chief. Johnson recalls how events in his life, such as his tour in Vietnam, graduating from college and joining the police force, have molded him into the man he is today.

(*Greenville News* **Article about Chief Willie Johnson**)

The marketplace in Hong Kong helped me realize that people around the world eat quite differently than Americans, especially the Hong Kong consumption of fish and chicken. They killed, chopped, and hung the chickens outside to air dry, a malodorous practice for certain. They used the same practice with fish. However, the diet in Vietnam was mostly rice, and sometimes the Vietnamese were fortunate enough to have a little fish. Overweight persons were a rarity in both places.

In December of 1969, I returned to the United States for leave. I was home for about three or four weeks before my next assignment in Fort Hood, Texas. While in Texas, I served as a recruitment sergeant for the military, required to recruit at least two soldiers monthly as a quota. A sergeant, offering me a tip on how I could meet my quota, suggested I get to know the soldiers well so that I knew who had financial challenges. Soldiers received a bonus payment for reenlisting in the army. As a result of his advice, I met my monthly quota and stayed in Texas until June 30, 1970, which completed my three-year military service.

After departing the military, I bought my first car, a 1970 Chevelle Super Sport 396 in ash gold with white-lettered tires and a stripe on the hood. I was in euphoria, and I became a well-sought-after bachelor. If you were not popular and you had a new car in Laurens, all the girls liked you. Even though the car did not have an air conditioner or powered windows, I was riding in a new car. I purchased that Chevelle from Milam Chevrolet and paid three thousand dollars. I paid one thousand dollars down and financed the other two.

While in Texas, the Metropolitan Police Force came to Fort Hood recruiting police officers. Candidates were given physicals and exams. I had learned to type and passed the test, so the Washington, DC Metropolitan Police Force hired me in May 1970. I was scheduled to report to work on September 5, 1970.

Because I had moved up so quickly to the rank of Staff Sergeant E6, my first sergeant was certain I was going to remain in the military. I, however, knew I was not. I was proud of my military career. I was decorated with the Bronze Star Medal (for gallantry in action and the ability to boost the morale of those who served with me), a South Vietnam Campaign Ribbon, an Air Medal, and a Combat Assault Award. While these were wonderful accolades, the structure and the rigidity of the military were not for me. I longed for a more relaxed life.

At the end of June, I returned home to Laurens. During my stay, I visited Greenville and happened to visit the Greenville Police Department on Broad Street. My desire was to expand my knowledge of policing because what I knew was limited. The first person I spotted was the police chief, and he asked if I needed help. I explained I had just gotten out of the military and accepted a job in Washington as a police officer. I wanted to know more about police officers' job descriptions. The chief took me into his office and after learning more about my military career, he was so impressed he asked if I were interested in a job with the Greenville Police Department. I reminded him I already had a job. He insisted I did not need to go to Washington to be a police officer.

I left the police department and returned to Laurens. The next morning, the police chief called and asked me to return to Greenville to talk to him again. I met with him the following day, and his strategy was to convince me to take the job by saying that I might be the future police chief. I was thinking to myself "I do not want to be a chief." Then, I thought about it. If I took the job and worked for a month, I could gain valuable experience I could use in DC. So, I took the job.

When I told my mother I had taken a job in DC, she cried because she did not want me to go. She said DC was a big town and I did not know anybody there. She did not think I would survive, so she tried to convince me it was not the right thing for me to do.

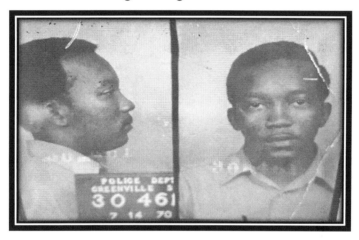

(First Work Photograph of Willie Johnson)

Needless to say, I stayed on the job in Greenville at the end of July. I almost quit the first month because of the racist attitudes I encountered. Another officer tried to convince me to stay by saying that the officer who used the racist slurs had problems and the other officers were not that way. He assured me I would do well, so I stayed. But instead of staying for a month, I stayed for 444 months (thirty-seven years). Later on, I found out that the Greenville Police Department had six Black officers out of a total of ninety. As I stated earlier, timing can mean everything in your life. Officer Eustace. E. Bennett transferred from the police department to the housing authority. He was the first Black officer hired by the GPD in 1964.

(E. E. Bennett, First Black Police Officer in Greenville, SC)

The police chief had his training assistant take me to see the chairperson of the Greenville Civil Service Commission. He interviewed me, whereby asking me to name at least ten businesses on Main Street. I think I named two and I told him I was a country boy from Laurens. He said that sounded like a pretty good answer, so I guess that meant I passed. He had several more questions concerning how I would react if a White person requested that I not come into their business. My response was if I was dispatched to the location and the person decided he did not really want the police, then I had no problem. However, I knew what he was hinting at. Many people had race issues in the early 1970's. Some linger today.

Bennett, who was mentioned earlier, left the police department in 1970. He was hired on January 1, 1964, and he paved the way for Blacks who served the Greenville Police Department after him. I met Officer Bennett, and we became good friends over the years. He shared that when he joined the department, his assignment was on Spring Street, where most Black businesses in the heart of Greenville were located. I give a special salute to him and his family for the sacrifices they made.

Throughout my law enforcement career, I wore many hats. I started in 1970 as a patrolman walking Main Street for a short time. In December of that same year, I moved out of my mother's house and rented a room at the YMCA in Greenville. I stayed there until my days off when I returned to Laurens. I worked many side jobs and stayed connected to the community. I recall working record hops at the Bernie Street YWCA for ten dollars. I worked security during the Monday night wrestling shows at the Greenville Memorial Auditorium, for Myers Arnold Department Store, Stuart's Ladies Dress Shop and high school basketball and football games. I also served as Chief of Security for Haywood Mall Shopping Center. I wanted my family to have nice things, and side jobs funded this goal.

Around March 1971, I rented an apartment in Nicholtown, where I paid seventy-two dollars a month. I purchased three rooms of furniture from Kimbrell's Furniture Company for nine hundred dollars. My mother and aunt provided me with curtains, and I was out on my own.

After a year and a half, in 1972, the police department decided to formulate the Metropolitan Narcotics Squad in response to the drug problems in Greenville. Heroin had become a popular drug. This was a joint task force of city, county, and state officers working under Solicitor Tom Greene. I was chosen to become a member of the squad and was assigned as a drug investigator. Later, I was promoted to detective, working general investigations and any other assignment I was given. I was often told that I was one of the best "cracker-jack" investigators. Each month, an arrest and clearance report were posted on the bulletin board, and I was always among the top three for performance.

Although I was enrolled at LaSalle University in Chicago, Illinois at the time, I decided that the criminal justice program at Greenville Technical College was better for me. Therefore, I enrolled and finished the program in 1975 with an associate degree. I was fortunate enough to later attend Southern Wesleyan University using the GI Bill and complete my bachelor's degree in Human Resources.

(WL Johnson, Narcotics Detective)

In late 1975, I was promoted to sergeant in the uniform patrol division as a squad leader. This required me to directly supervise a group of seven to ten police officers. Everything worked out well for me, and in 1976 I was promoted to lieutenant over a patrol platoon. This promotion made me the highest-ranking Black officer in the department. Chief Harold Jennings brought me into his office and told me that one of the officers on the platoon I would be assigned had made a racial remark about me. Chief Jennings did not tell me who the officer was and that he was not going to stand for anything like that. He advised me to just do my job. He told me he had full confidence in my ability to get the job done. His support made me dig deep and work harder.

I loved my time with the Metropolitan Narcotics Squad working undercover and making numerous drug arrests. The job was motivating and challenging. Bobby Brown, my first police partner, was a smart guy who shared tricks with me about how to police. He told me that all the drug dealers had money and girls migrated to guys with money. He also said drug dealers often had more than one girlfriend. If I became acquainted with the drug dealers' girlfriends and convinced them the guys were cheaters, the girlfriends would get mad at the guys and tell me everything. This tactic served me well.

(Greenville Police Department Promotions)

(Captain Richard Davis and Lieutenant Willie Johnson)

As a shift commander, it was important that I was supported in making changes for the betterment of the city. For example, there was a strong nightlife challenge occurring around the Washington Street area downtown that involved prostitution. I suggested to the chief that we target the "Johns" (men soliciting for sex), along with the female prostitutes. He gave me the go-ahead, and I met with three female officers from different platoons and one from the county. We set up a reverse sting on the men soliciting sex. The first night we arrested over one hundred men and about ten females. Needless to say, this operation was a complete success. We continued this process on and off until we drove street prostitution from the downtown area of the central business district. Because prostitution reverse stings worked so well, when I took over as captain over detectives, we continued with reverse drug stings.

When I was first promoted to platoon lieutenant in 1977, some of the officers on my shift felt I needed to prove myself to them. They wanted to know if I was able to do the job and if I would look out for them. It took me a few months, but I won them over. Knowing that both my shift and I were being watched, I kept my finger on the pulse. I radioed decisions to officers when they answered a call, and I answered calls with officers. I worked double time with my officers. I felt that more was expected of me; therefore, I went the extra mile.

As a platoon lieutenant, each year there was a competition during the Brace-A-Child campaign (BAC). For this program, law enforcement across the state partnered with restaurants to raise money to purchase leg braces for crippled children. Each patrol platoon competed to raise the most money for the Easter Seal Society. My platoon became very aggressive and won this competition almost every year. Then, officers were highly motivated, even entering bars and nightspots to sell the BAC buttons. They stayed until many times the owners did not want the police around. Just joking! Anyway, I instilled the concept of teamwork within my officers.

Things were going well for my patrol platoon, and we were efficient. Then, a complaint came in from a sergeant on another shift that my people were lazy and sleeping on the third shift. The patrol captain called me into his office and confronted me with this allegation. I was upset and responded by telling him to check the arrest record and the break-in reports for the past year.

The records showed that my platoon had more arrests and fewer breaking and entering cases than the other two. As fate would have it, that report put this backstabbing incident to rest quickly.

My path would not work for everyone. It was important to me to share a significant amount of time with my officers off duty. We had a platoon softball team, playing against each other and against other platoons. We also played basketball and were very competitive. Additionally, one of my sergeants was a die-hard deer hunter, and as many as twenty-five of us hunted together. We entered the woods as early as 5:00 AM to hunt deer. Friendship and comradery were built between officers and supervisors. When I was promoted to captain, the officers presented me with a plaque for my leadership as the commander of the "Blue Machine Platoon."

The army taught me that relationships are important, because as the saying goes, "People don't care how much you know until they know how much you care." The vast cultural experiences I was afforded are difficult to even describe. His Excellency, Samuel Ernest Quarm, Ambassador from Ghana to the United States, visited Greenville in March 1975. My partner,

Harold Beeks, and I were assigned to provide security for him, protecting him from kidnap, assassination, or other dangerous situations often faced by dignitaries.

(Left to Right—Rev. Dr. John Corbitt, Detective Willie Johnson, Quarm's Assistant, Ambassador Samuel Quarm, Detective Dorothy Butler, and Detective Harold Beeks)

True Stories of Over 100 Years…

THE CITY OF GREENVILLE, SOUTH CAROLINA

MAX M. HELLER   OFFICE OF THE MAYOR

February 19, 1976

Sergeant W. L. Johnson
Greenville City Police Department
Greenville, South Carolina 29602

Dear Sergeant Johnson:

Chief Jennings has made me aware that you originated and implemented the idea of the City/County basketball game for the Bennett/Calloway Benefit Fund.

This was a wonderful project and we are very proud to know that our officers are initiating this type of activity.

Please thank all of those who have been involved in this project and a special thanks to you.

Sincerely,

Max M. Heller
Mayor

MMH:bcc

cc: Mr. John J. Dullea
     Chief Harold Jennings

(Letter of Commendation from Mayor Max Heller to Detective Willie Johnson)

In 1976, Greg Bennett, a young man at Greenville High School, was injured while making a tackle in a football game. Unfortunately, he was paralyzed. During that same time, another young man named Todd Calloway was injured in a gym accident. I was a sergeant and suggested to Chief Harold Jennings that law enforcement show support for these young men. He agreed. I set up a benefit basketball game between the city police and the county sheriff's office. We raised eight hundred dollars and divided the gate proceeds between the families of those two men.

I received a commendation letter from Mayor Max Heller for organizing this benefit basketball game. Coincidentally, years later, Tammy Calloway, the sister of Todd Calloway, began working for the police department as a dispatcher on my platoon.

True Stories of Over 100 Years…

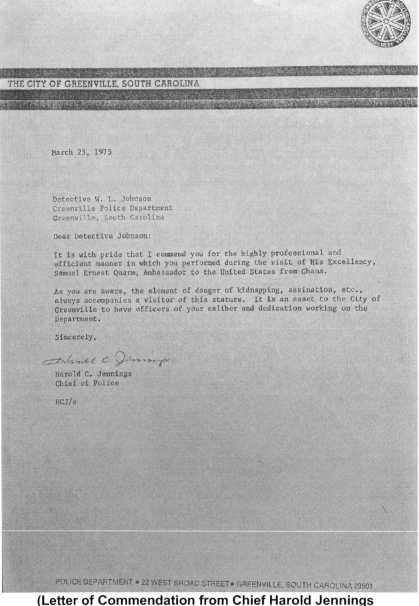

(Letter of Commendation from Chief Harold Jennings to Detective Willie Johnson)

True Stories of Over 100 Years…

Deputies Lose; 2 Youths Win

The Greenville Police Department beat the Greenville County Sheriff's Department in basketball Thursday night, but Todd Calloway and Greg Bennett were the real winners.

The benefit game earned $800 for the funds for the two youths. Calloway was critically injured in a gym accident and Bennett was paralyzed during a high school football game.

The city won the basketball game at Wade Hampton High School, 63 to 60 in overtime. During the game 14 players for the city saw action and 10 county players.

The county players reportedly included a highway patrolman who was "really cleaning the backboards," a city policeman said. The city policeman said the county was winning by as much as 12 points up until the last quarter.

Two high school coaches officiated during the first half and detention officer Jackie Gardo and another coach officiated in the second half.

The game was organized by Lt. Carl Foster of the Greenville County Sheriff's Department and Sgt. W.J. Johnson of the Greenville Police Department.

"Local law enforcement is concerned about the community they live in," Johnson said. "We are interested in the welfare of the children who will be the adult community of the future."

Defendant Gets 3-Year Sentence

Matthew Harper, 45, was sentenced to three years imprisonment, suspended to three years probation and $500 after pleading guilty in General Sessions Court Thursday to assault and battery of a high and aggravated nature.

In other court action, Julian Scott, 50, was sentenced to one year or $1,000, suspended to three months and one year probation after a jury found him guilty of driving under the influence.

Trial began for Robert Lee Wright, 25, who is charged with failure to return a rented vehicle. Testimony is scheduled to continue Friday.

(*Greenville News* Article on Police Sponsored Benefit Basketball Game)

In 1977, a Greenville sergeant on my platoon was shot in the leg while serving a search warrant at an illegal liquor house. There was an uproar in the community as a result. One of the community leaders initiated a meeting with the chief of police to discuss the need to broker a better relationship between the Black community in West Greenville and law enforcement. Chief Jennings, my mentor, approached me again and said we needed to organize positive activities with the young people. I set up a basketball team coached by police officers, and I served as one of the coaches. This created a great relationship between the West Greenville Community with law enforcement. I recall that some years later, I met one of the girls who was on the team, and she had become a nurse. She thanked the police for being a positive image during her teen years.

In 1982 when Mayor Jesse L. Helms died, I was asked to select officers to serve as a Color and Honor Guard presenting the American and state flags at his funeral. My military background and prior training as a drill sergeant made me a perfect fit for the assignment. The department started a Color Guard Unit, which is still active today.

In 1987, I was promoted to captain over investigations, which made me the first Black captain in the history of the Greenville Police Department. My wife and church family held a celebration for me that was attended by over two hundred people. My promotion offered hope within the Black community in upstate South Carolina.

Johnson could become first black police captain

The Greenville Police Department will have its first black captain if the city's Civil Service Commisssion approves the nomination of Lt. W.L. Johnson at its meeting tonight.

Chief Mike Bridges said today that Johnson, currently the highest-ranking black officer on the force, was nominated from the department's six lieutenants. Assisting Bridges in the selection were the current police captains. Johnson will be interviewed by the civil service commissioners tonight.

"I feel real good about Johnson's nomination," Bridges said. He added that any of the six lieutenants would have made a good choice, but he thought Johnson was the right choice for now.

Johnson is a watch commander in the uniform patrol division and has worked as a detective in the past, Bridges said.

Bridges said Johnson began his service with the Police Department in July 1970 after serving in the U.S. Army. He is a native of Laurens.

Bridges said if Johnson were confirmed, he would become captain of the detective division, which Bridges headed until he was appointed chief in September, replacing the retiring Harold Jennings.

Bridges said interviews also will be conducted later this week to fill a sergeant position and a lieutenant position left vacant through the promotions.

(*Greenville News* Article about Johnson's Promotion as First Black Captain)

True Stories of Over 100 Years…

W.L. Johnson named first black captain

The promotion of W.L. Johnson by the city's Civil Service Commission Monday night gives the Greenville Police Department its first black captain.

Johnson, who as a lieutenant was the the highest-ranking black officer on the force, was chosen from the department's six lieutenants. Police Chief Mike Bridges said he and the other police captains made the selection.

Johnson

Johnson will become the commander of the Detective Division, which Bridges headed until he was appointed chief in September. Johnson is a watch commander in the Uniform Patrol Division, but also has worked as a detective, Bridges said.

(*Greenville News* Article about Johnson's Promotion as First Black Captain)

Later in 1995, I received another promotion. I was elevated to the rank of major, which made me the first major in the history of the Greenville Police Department. This made me the deputy chief. Because many people had confidence in me, I had to work even harder to not disappoint. I set goals for the investigation's division, and we all pushed hard. Everything was not always the way it should be. I had to be the fixer in some incidents where officers stepped over the line. We had an officer overreact once when a citizen pointed her finger into his face. He grabbed her finger and twisted and dislocated it. I met with this lady, and we came to a resolution that we would pay her medical bills. She was content.

On another occasion, a supervisor gave officers the go-ahead to kick in a door without a search warrant when they were attempting to serve a warrant. The subject they were looking for was not present, and the officers confiscated a personal photograph from the homeowner. The homeowner reported the incident, and again, I met with the individual. We agreed that the police department was wrong, I offered an apology and we repaired the door. Our job is to operate (between the lines) and keep the entire community safe. I learned the phrase, "when you mess up, 'fess up and then clean up."

After serving as a patrolman, detective, sergeant, lieutenant, captain, and major for over 30 years at the Greenville Police Department, I was appointed Chief of Police in 2000. This was the most significant highlight in my career. I became the 23rd Chief of Police in Greenville, SC, a position I held until I retired in 2007. The chiefs of police since 1845 are listed as follows:

1845 – 1852	JAMES GOODLET
1852 – 1854	WILLIAM HARRISON
1854 – 1855	JOHN T. A. McDANIEL
1855 – 1856	FULLER GOPELT
1856 – 1863	Z. MARTIN
1864 – 1870	T. GOSETT
1870 – 1871	J.L. KENNING
1871 – 1872	AMBER BATSON
1873 – 1884	JOHN G. GREER
1885 – 1890	R.H. KENNEDY
1891 – 1892	J. P. LIGON
1893 – 1906	R. H. KENNEDY
1907 – 1908	MR. ALTMAN
1908 – 1911	R. H. KENNEDY
1911 – 1915	J. E. HOLCOMBE

True Stories of Over 100 Years…

1915 – 1921	J. D. NOE
1921 – 1944	J. E. SMITH
1944 – 1955	J. H. JENNINGS
1956 – 1968	P. P. OAKES
1968 – 1975	E. N. NORRIS
1975 – 1987	H. C. JENNINGS
1987 – 2000	D. M. BRIDGES
2000 – 2007	W. L. JOHNSON

True Stories of Over 100 Years…

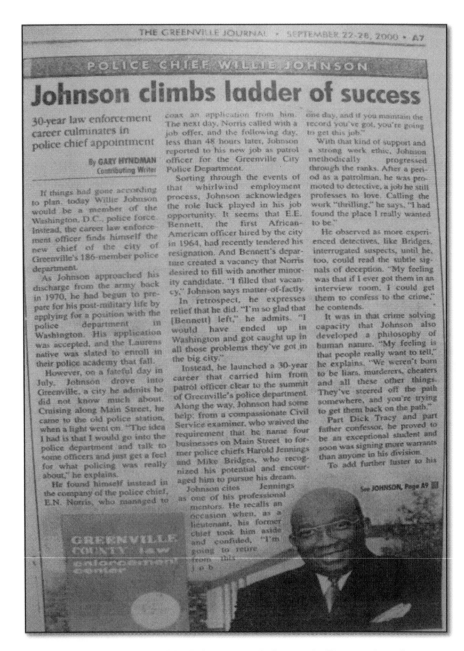

(*Greenville Journal* Article about Johnson's Promotions)

True Stories of Over 100 Years…

Captain Kelley
Military & Early Career

True Stories of Over 100 Years…

True Stories of Over 100 Years...

After I graduated from high school in 1965, I was drafted. I was sent to an army recruiting station at Fort Jackson in Columbia, SC, where I began boot camp. I assumed at that time I was in the United States Army. However, during processing I was sent to a large tin building known as a Quonset Hut along with some other recruits. When I entered the hut, I noticed there were military personnel from every branch of the military: the Marine Corps, Air Force, Navy, and Army, standing in front of us on a platform.

Each branch's representative spoke to the group. The Marine representative asked for ten volunteers for the United States Marine Corps. Quite naturally, I thought no one wanted to volunteer for the Marines because it was known as the toughest branch of service you could enter. At the time of the representative's proposal, I did not have any fear of being selected because I was skin and bones. I probably weighed one hundred and fifteen pounds soaking wet. I was a small guy. As I predicted, no one raised their hand to volunteer.

The recruits lined up in formation and the next thing I knew, I saw all of the guys moving aside. It reminded me of Moses parting the Red Sea. I noticed the Marine representative coming directly toward me. He looked me dead in the eyes and started asking me what was on my face. I was nervous at this point. At the time, I had started trying to grow a mustache. The representative made the statement that by zero nine hundred hours, I was going to have that shaved off of my face. He continued by saying, "Do you understand me, Marine?" When he said that, both of my knees were shaking, and I soon realized that I was headed to the Marines. The Marine representative pointed to a designated area for me to stand. I found out later that the Marines were trying to meet a quota by enlisting a certain number of minorities.

Later that night, after the representative recruited eight or nine additional young men, he loaded us on a bus, and we traveled from Fort Jackson to Beaufort, South Carolina's Parris Island Marine Corps Recruit Depot. During the trip inside the dark bus, I could hear some of the guys crying. Truth be told, I probably should have been crying myself. Early in the morning, we finally reached Parris Island, with its golden arches at the entrance that looked like those at McDonald's. When the bus stopped, another drill instructor boarded the bus and started calling us every demeaning name he could think of. He was intimidating and at that point, I felt I had died and gone to hell.

During my time at Parris Island, I realized if a person showed any sign of weakness, things would get difficult for the person. It appeared that those in charge tried to do everything they could to keep us from completing boot camp at Parris Island. They tore you down as a person to instill discipline in you. My motivation for making it through was not wanting to disappoint my father, a World War II veteran. I wanted to make him proud of me no matter what I had to go through. I spent eight weeks training at Parris Island, realizing how much better White recruits were treated over Blacks and minorities.

As graduation day approached, a number of my fellow Marines mentioned their families were coming to see them graduate, but I knew how difficult it might have been financially for my mother and father to make the trip. Actually, it was okay because I did not want them to see me in the condition that I was in at the time.

The day after graduation, we were loaded on a bus and sent to Camp LeJeune, North Carolina, for advanced training II. We had basic training at Camp Geiger in the areas in which we were to specialize. My area was infantry. At some point, I was asked what I wanted to specialize in, and I chose to be a machine gunner. I became a conditioned, killing machine. After my training at Camp LeJeune, I was given boot leave and allowed to return home for a couple of weeks.

After boot leave, my father and mother drove me to the Greenville-Spartanburg International Airport, and I reported to Camp Pendleton, California. Experiencing some firsts, such as flying on a plane and traveling to California kept me excited. When I arrived at Camp Pendleton, I joined the Third Battalion 26th Marines.

Once we had trained for many weeks, we boarded a ship en route to Vietnam. On the way to Vietnam, we made stops in Hawaii, Okinawa, and the Philippines to train for about a month and a half. The terrain in these areas was similar to the terrain we would be subjected to in Vietnam.

Aboard the aircraft carriers USS Iwo Jima and the USS Valley Forge, I made the journey to Vietnam. One night on the ship to Vietnam, a friend of mine told me he had just met a guy from Greenville. I told him there was no one on the ship from Greenville but me. He insisted he had met a guy from Greenville, so I asked to see him. We went down to a different part of the ship. When I saw this guy, I did not know his name, but I was very familiar with his face. He was from Greenville and had attended Washington High School. His name was John McIntyre, and we became incredibly good friends. We served in the same battalion, and when we were on operations, I could look across the rice paddy fields and distinguish John McIntyre from any other Marine because of his unique walk.

Once I arrived in Vietnam and experienced what all infantry personnel experience, my biggest problem was not the fear of the conditions or the possibility of being killed, but the fact that I was so homesick. I missed my mother, my father, and my girlfriend, who would later become my wife. Before I left Vietnam, I sent my wife's engagement ring home to my mother for safekeeping. I did not explain to my mother that it was a ring for my girlfriend, and my mother thought I was sending the ring to her. Needless to say, I had some explaining to do.

As a minority, I experienced a lot of racism, and that Blacks, Puerto Ricans, and other minorities were more closely knit than we were with the Whites. I often compared the "draft" to how our ancestors must have felt when they were taken from their home country against their will, brought to the United States and forced into slavery. I was around nineteen years old when I entered the Marines and being pulled away from home against my will was devastating. I never would have volunteered because of the possibility of going to Vietnam. Yet, there I was.

During my tour in Vietnam, I received a Purple Heart for being wounded by a Viet Cong Mortar Grenade. I suffered shrapnel in my leg, but more devastating was witnessing the killings of too many of my fellow Marines.

True Stories of Over 100 Years…

One of my happier memories of being in Vietnam came when we were in Khe Sahn, and my tour was ending. I had been unable to return home sooner because we were losing so many Marines. On that particular day, I was in a bunker, and I heard my First Sergeant from off in the distance say, "Listen up. I'm going to call some names and when I do, I want you to pack your bags." He called my name, and I knew I was going home. I was so happy I couldn't believe it. I had sent up many, many prayers at night telling the good Lord if He allowed me to make it home, He would not have to worry about me wanting to go anywhere else, ever.

To this day, my wife, who loves to travel, gets upset with me because I do not like going on vacation. I'll send her and make it nice for her, but I care nothing about traveling. I remember taking my wife to Hawaii because she had never been. Traveling across all of the water brought back memories of the day I left going to Vietnam.

I remember packing my bags and being transported from Khe Sahn to Da Nang Harbor. Then I boarded the USS John Pope, along with about three thousand other troops, and headed home. When the ship left Vietnam, I stood outside and watched Vietnam until it was the size of my fingertip, while saying to myself 'bye bye.'

The trip home took five to six days. Sailing home gave us time to reprogram our minds and to return our hygiene to order. While we were in the fields, we could not bathe or brush our teeth daily. Memories of the nightly talks with some of the other Marines as we sailed home are cherished.

Because US citizens were protesting the Vietnam War as well as the military personnel who traveled to Vietnam, our welcome home celebration that we were due was not what we received. As we pulled into San Diego Harbor, protestors were marching. It took about eight hours for us to be processed so we could depart the ship. We had to go through customs to make sure we were not bringing forbidden items into the US. Then, we received our orders. About three of us took a cab from San Diego to Los Angeles to connect with our flight home.

Sleeping during most of the plane trip home, upon landing John McIntyre and I assumed we were in Greenville. Eager to be home, we jumped up and headed off the plane. As we walked down the steps, we noticed how strangely things appeared. A flight attendant called from the top of the stairs to warn us that we were at the wrong stop. We were in Tennessee. Activating a little more patience, we returned to the plane and proceeded to the Greenville Spartanburg International Airport.

After our landing, John and I recognized a guy we knew working at the airport, and he was kind enough to give us a ride to my home. When we pulled up to my house, my mother was outside sweeping the porch. She knew I was due home; she just did not know when. Mom called my father and told him I was home, and he took a break from work to spend time with me. After spending a short time chatting, my father drove John home. I thanked God for bringing me home safely.

After leaving Vietnam, I still had some time left to serve in the Marines. I returned to Camp LeJeune, North Carolina, and served as a military policeman. That was when I started to consider law enforcement as a possible career.

When I left the military and returned home in 1968, I married the love of my life, and we have been married for 53 years. In the beginning it was not easy, but we had a strong support system. We both came from hard working families who instilled in us a great work ethic and the power of prayer. We lived with my mother-in-law, Mrs. Loney Riser, and the love and support she provided us, not to mention her wonderful meals, helped us establish a strong foundation for our future family. Joaquina and I have three beautiful children, a son, Calvin Jr., and two daughters, Rene' and LaShay. Working in law enforcement, so much family time is sacrificed when you must work side jobs to provide for your family, but we made it work. I am proud of each of my children.

Calvin Jr. is happily married and a supervisor with a company in SC. My daughter Rene is an investigator with the 13th Circuit Solicitor's Office. Although my youngest girl was nicknamed "Lil' Police Girl" by my brother Harold, she did not follow in my footsteps. LaShay is a proud mother and a Certified IT Analyst for a hospital system. I have also been blessed with six grandchildren and two great-grandchildren. Joaquina has been my biggest supporter during my career, and I do not know that I would have made it without her.

Fortunately, when you serve in the military, your workplace will hold your job for you upon your return. After my service, I returned to work at Stone

Manufacturing Company, where I had initially begun working because my father worked there many years before. I only stayed at that job for a short period before going to work at Fiber Industries, a polymer factory. I worked there for about a year and a half. One night, as I worked with my friend Harold Beeks, I told him I was thinking about joining the police department. Harold told me to let him know if I was successful because he might join me.

In 1970, I applied for employment at the Greenville City Police Department. I encountered an officer working in administration, and he instructed me to fill out the application. The first thing he told me was that I was too short. Well, the first thing that entered my mind was I had just served my country in Vietnam for the sake of keeping him safe, even enduring injuries while there, and here he was telling me that I was too short. He said he would check on things and let me know. He would be in touch.

Landing a job at the Greenville City Police Department was not an easy feat. I made five or six trips to the office to check on the job and eventually when I saw the officer in administration, he had this very disgusted look on his face. I could only imagine what he was thinking. Sadly, there were only five or six Black officers on the force.

On my final trip to check on my application, I ran into the officer in administration again wearing that same disgusted look on his face. The first thing out of his mouth was "Kelley, didn't I tell you that you are too short?" My gut told me to turn around and walk out. But just as I did, I encountered a White police officer coming in for the second shift. I had to look down at him; he was not as tall as I was. At that moment I spoke loudly and said, "Hold up. Wait a minute! I'm too short, so what is this I'm looking at? Your mascot?" I just knew I was going to jail that day. The officer who was shorter than me was looking at me wondering what in the world was going on. I got closer to him and wrote down his name and badge number. Overhearing the commotion, the administrative officer came out of his office and asked me to settle down. When he told me he would call me the next day, I told him, "No. The news probably wanted to hear about how I was too short, but it was okay for the other police officer." I left without another word.

The next day I received a call from the officer in administration. "Kelley, guess what? Come on up here.

We are going to give you the job." It was obvious that they had already checked my background and found that I was qualified. And apparently, I grew a few inches overnight.

Over the years, I became good friends with the officer who was shorter than me. Occasionally, my wife and I run into him, and he always wants me to tell the story about what happened that day at the police department. I always tell him that he is the reason I was able to get into law enforcement.

When I started at the Greenville City Police Department, there were so few Blacks in law enforcement. It was exciting to see one of the other Black officers, Willie Johnson, who started a few months before me, between shifts because we were never paired as partners. The same racism that attempted to exclude me from the department showed its ugly head during training and daily operations. Some of my trainers were so accustomed to using the 'N' word that they found it difficult to refrain from using it in my presence. Some of them used it just to harass us and see our reaction.

One particular night, I was assigned to front desk duty with the desk sergeant who was my senior by many years. Around one o'clock in the morning, a disoriented, homeless, black elderly female entered the police department. The White officer said, "What is this old nigger doing out at this time in the morning?" I was caught off guard and could not believe what I heard. My response was, "What did you say?" He looked at me and had the audacity to repeat what he had said. I said the quickest prayer I've ever said in my life to keep from doing something I would regret.

Immediately, I exited the counter area to help the poor lady because I did not want her to get close to the sergeant. I asked if I could help her. I think she was suffering from some form of dementia, and I called someone to pick her up. I just knew I did not want that sergeant to have any dealings with her. He had already shown me the type of person he was by what he had said.

During my time in the department, I continuously encountered similar ordeals. Daily, before we hit our beats, we had a roll call. We gathered in a room and stood around as the supervisor in charge told us what was going on that day, what outstanding warrants there were, and what BOLOs (things to be looking out for) during our shift. There was not a roll call that I remember where one of the White officers did not let the word 'nigger' come out of their mouths. It became such a constant thing. It made my fellow Black officers and me wonder what types of things were said when we were not around. During that time, I'm surprised none of us Black officers were targeted to be killed. There were so many prejudiced officers, you never knew who actually had your back.

Occurrences similar to those at the Greenville Police Department were also experienced at the Greenville Fire Department. So many Whites did not want Blacks in either place. Instead of things progressing since I retired in 1999, it seems those departments are taking steps backward when it comes to representation. My fellow Black officers and I grew weary. We reached a point where we started challenging the wrongdoings. Even during that time, we would not just sit and listen when one of them said anything derogatory. We called them out and let them know it was offensive.

Once when I responded to a domestic call at the home of a White couple, the husband had beaten his wife who was all bloody in the face from being punched in the nose. My partner was a White officer at the time.

Upon our exiting the car, the first thing this lady said was, "That nigger police can't come in my house, but you are welcome," referring to the White officer. He showed me who he was that day. He said to the lady, "Let me tell you something. This officer is here to help you. If he can't come into your house, then I can't come into your house." Some of the other officers would have reacted differently, but I was grateful for my partner's response.

About two years into my career at the Greenville City Police Department, a very highly regarded sergeant who was well aware of the racism Black officers encountered approached me. He shared that he knew what I was dealing with, and that the climate would change if I just hung in there. He promised. Apparently, I had given him a reason to think I was considering leaving. His coming to me and expressing his concerns showed me that all Whites are not prejudiced.

While responding to a burglar alarm call one day, I saw a man driving a Winnebago with a lot of campaign slogans promoting 'Cash Williams for Sheriff.' Mr. Williams, the driver, approached me and said he was going to need some qualified Black officers when he became sheriff. He asked if I would consider working for him. I asked him what he had to offer. He asked what I wanted, and I specifically informed him that I wanted to work in vice and narcotics. At the time, no one thought there was any chance of Williams defeating the current sheriff. Mr. Williams said if I worked for him when he became sheriff, he would give me exactly what I wanted. He would also make sure I got a brand-new car every year. I thought to myself, this man is making some big promises, and I did not think any more about it.

About two months later, I was watching the election results on TV and sure enough, Cash Williams was elected sheriff. The following day, another officer he had recruited from the Greenville City Police called me and asked if I remembered the conversation I had with Cash Williams. I told him, "Yes." Then, he asked if I was planning to work for him. I told him if Mr. Williams gave me what I asked for then I sure would work for him. Not long after, I was advised to turn in my resignation with two weeks' notice, which I did.

A few days later, after giving my letter to the Greenville City Police Department, the chief and lieutenant called and asked me to come in. As I walked in, ironically, the chief and lieutenant were gathered in the same hallway where I kept being turned down by that administrator. They said if I stayed, I would be the first Black sergeant. I knew then they wanted to keep their quota. My mind was already made up. After two weeks, I was out of there. I joined the Greenville County Sheriff's Office and everything that Sheriff Williams promised me, he delivered.

True Stories of Over 100 Years…

Captain Harper
Military & Early Career

True Stories of Over 100 Years…

True Stories of Over 100 Years...

During my junior and senior high school years, my mindset was to serve in the military. I knew I would not be attending college immediately after high school. And I certainly knew I didn't want to work in a mill. I preferred a military job that would translate into a civilian occupation following my military career. I thought volunteering for the army instead of waiting to be drafted would increase my chances of being assigned to an army occupation of my choice. Oops! My first choice was a military police officer. That did not happen. My next choice was to be a photographer. I fell in love with photography when I received a Kodak Brownie Hawkeye camera on my twelfth or thirteenth birthday. Unfortunately, I would not be an army photographer either.

My military assignment was infantryman with the MOS (military occupational status) Eleven Bravo. I learned later it was commonly called "11-Bang-Bang." With that MOS, I served as a rifleman, trained to seek out and kill the enemy. I was so disappointed about not getting one of the MOS's I requested. I was sure the army recruiters said I would get one of the two jobs I asked for if I volunteered. That infantry MOS would not translate to a civilian career unless I became a hitman for the mob. This MOS also meant more than likely; I would see combat in a war zone. And if I weren't in a war zone, I would be in the boonies playing war games.

While on a long march during my third or fourth week of basic training, I saw my high school friend, Gettis, aka "Meatball." I looked him up after our march. He was in another battalion, and I learned he had enlisted a week or two after I had. We later communicated and vowed to stay in touch. We swapped letters for a while but eventually lost touch. I did not see him again until after we had left the military.

In September, after graduating from basic training,

I was sent to Fort Knox, Kentucky, for AIT (Advanced Infantry Training). While participating in an overnight field training exercise in November or December, I suffered a mild case of frostbite on both feet. Before Christmas, 1966, I completed AIT training and returned home on leave.

My next military orders were to South Korea. I felt fortunate that I had avoided Vietnam. Although the situation in Korea was not as intense as in Vietnam, it was still war. Going to Korea would be my first flying experience. As an 18-year-old on a 14-hour flight and leaving the United States brought about a barrage of emotions. I was scared, nervous, and excited all at the same time.

Winters in Korea can be extremely harsh. My assigned area was near the DMZ (Demilitarized Zone), aka "the Z," which is the border that divides North Korea from South Korea. We rode in personnel carriers within a mile or two to our stakeout locations and walked the remainder of the way. We wore thermal boots, aka "Mickey Mouse boots," that caused our feet to sweat. These boots were constructed of layers of rubber with wool insulation between them, designed to prevent heat from escaping while preventing cold air from penetrating the outer rubber layers. Once we reached our bunkers, right before dark, we remained there until just after sunrise. As a result of the cold and after perspiring from walking, our feet would freeze inside our boots.

Our assignment's goal along that river was to prevent the enemy from crossing over into South Korea. There, I pulled stakeout and ambush patrols along the Imjin River. My feet were again frostbitten, still not severely, but enough that I wanted no part of Korea's bitter winters. (To this day, I still suffer from those cold-weather injuries.)

During frigid winters along the Imjin River that separates South and North Korea, the enemy donned clothing to blend in with snow and ice. Then they simply walked across the frozen river into S. Korea. We set out trip flares and Claymore mines in the stakeout positions along the riverfront. My daily prayers were to live to see another day and return stateside with all of my limbs. We were in the dark, and when flares tripped, they lit up the entire area. On most occasions, we didn't see the enemy, just the result of the enemy. We started shooting in the direction of the tripped flare, and the enemy returned fire. Also, the Claymore was sometimes turned around 180 degrees toward us. Every day I survived was a blessing and gift!

Our company usually spent three consecutive weeks on the Z and a week in the rear. Korea was a hardship tour; therefore, we received extra pay for serving in a hazardous duty zone. Occasionally, I was assigned as unit police when back at our company compound. This job was as close as I came to law enforcement during my military career.

Spending months away from my family was difficult, and I longed to see them again. Other than letters, I had no contact with them for about 14 months. Sending money to my mother back home brought me a little comfort during this deployment.

While in Korea, I purchased my first professional camera, a 35mm Petri FT, SLR, which I still cherish. I spent most of my spare time photographing and playing pool or table tennis. I traveled to other military units trying to find pool players. I met only two other soldiers in Korea who were far better pool players than me, one each from Chicago and Pennsylvania.

The standard length of a Korean tour was thirteen months. A few months near the end of hazardous duty assignments, soldiers are required to complete what is known by soldiers as a "dream sheet." It is a form of three choices of military bases where the soldier wants to be assigned. I completed the form listing Fort Jackson, South Carolina, Fort Gordon, Georgia, and Fort Belvoir, Virginia, as my choices, hoping to be assigned closer to home.

(Harper Pictured as a Unit Police in Korea)

Well, guess where my next assignment was? Germany. That's correct, Germany. I would say the name "dream sheet" is appropriate. That wasn't the worst part. As I got close to the end of my tour, I had pleasant surprises while clearing the post for leaving Korea. Within a span of two weeks, I met three people from Laurens in villages frequented by soldiers. One was a classmate, Frankie Jones. We walked past each other for a few steps, turned around, and I said, "Frankie." He said, "Harp." We stood and talked for about thirty minutes before going our separate ways.

The North Koreans soon seized the U.S. Naval Intelligence Vessel, the Pueblo. They captured and held the crew of American sailors hostage. I received word that the army canceled my orders to leave Korea. Therefore, I ended up spending about a month longer in Korea.

I arrived in Germany in April 1968. In many ways, Germany was vastly different from Korea. However, the winters were similar. It snowed in May, the month after I arrived. At least half of my time was spent in training, playing war games. I slept under the stars and in the elements many nights, trying to prevent my body's temperature from dropping to dangerous levels by hovering over the engine exhaust of a tank or personnel carrier. My experience in the army is why I'm not too fond of camping today. Most outdoor photographers camp near an area to get that scenic sunrise shot. I'd rather sleep indoors in a comfortable bed and get up a couple of hours early and hike to be there at sunrise.

Shortly after arriving in Germany, I advanced to the rank of Sergeant E-5. This promotion allowed me to have private quarters, a perk which I relished—no longer having to bunk in a room with other soldiers. Having my own space would also allow me to follow through with a business I'd been thinking of. Payday was around the first of the month. Some G.I.'s were notorious for gambling and losing it all, often within a few days of getting paid. Then they would borrow from other soldiers. I had a plan to help them out. I put a metal barred double-wall locker in my room. It would hold the pawn items I required when a G.I. lost his money and needed a loan until the next payday. I was open for business! If they wanted a loan, the interest rate was 25 to 50 cents on the dollar.

True Stories of Over 100 Years...

(Sergeant Harper on Desk Duty)

The main reason for enlisting in the army was to find a better way of life for myself and to see places I may not otherwise have seen. The army afforded me opportunities to visit Japan, Greece, Korea, Germany, Austria, and other European countries. While in Greece, on a training exercise in a remote area, we encountered people who had never seen Black people. Some asked to touch us to see if our dark color would rub off. Like all other places I visited, I played pool in Greece during my downtime. Only there, it wasn't called pool. It was known as "Carom Billiards," and to me, it is more complicated. The larger, pocketless pool tables led to a vastly different and undesirable experience, but I played anyway.

On June 30, 1969, at Fort Dix, New Jersey, I received my honorable discharge from the military. When I enlisted into the service, I was a teenager, and I considered myself to have grown into manhood upon leaving. The military experience, and Germany in particular, was pretty good for me. While stationed there, I bought a new car through the military's new car purchase program.

On my way home to South Carolina, I stopped in DC to visit my father. I then rode the Greyhound bus from Washington, DC to Laurens. After relaxing for a week, a friend drove me to Charleston to pick up my new car. It was great being around family and getting reacquainted with friends. A friend approached me with the business idea of opening a club together. It wasn't really a club, more like a teen hangout. We shared the rent; he was the D.J. and provided beverages and snacks for reselling. I provided the music and related equipment.

When I left the military, the Vietnam War was winding down. There were talks of possibly ending the military draft, leading to a significant decrease in National Guard enlistments. They were conducting a robust recruiting drive. I received an offer that included a recruiting position with the liberty to recruit as I saw fit. They only wanted results. I retained my army rank as a sergeant with the promise of a promotion. The pay was decent, so I signed on. We drilled one weekend a month in Laurens at the National Guard Armory. I was assigned a jeep, and I drove to wherever I thought I could enlist people. And yes, I spent some time, actually a lot of time, recruiting in pool rooms.

Within thirty days of my discharge, I took a full-time job working at The Laurens Glass Factory. However, I did not like the rotating shifts and the manual labor. That job was for me to stand at the end of a conveyor belt and place crates of bottles from the belt onto a pallet. After about three weeks, I walked off the job on a Friday afternoon. On that Friday, for most of the day, I'd been in a nine-ball pool game on the front table, doing extremely well. As a single 21-year-old, I didn't have any real debt. Why was I going to work on the second shift on a Friday afternoon? Reluctantly, I left the pool room and reported to work at the glass factory. I couldn't help but think about what I left in the pool room and Friday night possibilities. With those thoughts, I left work without notifying anyone and went straight to the pool room. I never returned for my pay, and I don't recall ever getting it. I did not seek another job for a while.

I'd decided when I did return to work that I would seek a first shift job. The Torrington Plant hired me in a manual labor position. I started networking right away, trying to move to a non-manual labor position. I had conversations with electricians and other maintenance workers about moving into a more desirable job that paid better. After talking to my supervisor and human resources personnel, human resources promised me an electrician's job if I attended school and received the required training and certification.

After enrolling at Greenville Technical College to take industrial electronics classes, I moved to the second shift. That class wasn't taught in the evening, only during the day. The one-year program prepared students for most industrial employers, such as Michelin, Duke Energy, Bell South, and General Electric. Students often were hired before graduating. I felt comfortable with my knowledge and credentials and anticipated becoming an electrician at Torrington.

After graduation, I returned to HR and learned there were no openings in maintenance. A few weeks later, I was still on the second shift when I saw a teenager with an electrician's tool pouch strapped to his side. I began a conversation with him and learned he had just graduated from high school. That was enough for Torrington to hire him as an OJT electrician. In addition, he said they were paying for his tuition to attend Piedmont Technical College.

At that point, I decided to leave Laurens. I called in sick for the next few days at Torrington. I applied for employment at Bell South, Duke Power, and several other locations in Greenville. I also applied for a job with the police department and the South Carolina Highway Patrol.

Upon returning to Torrington, my supervisor summoned me to his office. When I arrived, the department head was with my supervisor, and they said someone from the Greenville Police Department was on the phone and wished to speak with me. They stayed in the office while I took the phone call, and their faces made it apparent they thought I was in trouble.

Ironically, the Greenville Police Department was offering me a job. I had done well on the background investigation and testing, and they wanted me to start within a few weeks. I verbally accepted the position during the call. I informed my supervisor and the department head I would be leaving, and neither responded. But, before my shift was over, that information was all over my department. I was also offered a job at Bell South around the same time but declined it.

On the second shift, my official start date with The Greenville Police Department was Saturday, January 5, 1974. However, sometime before the start date, I reported to the police pistol range. The Police Clubhouse was under construction. While I did receive some firearm training, it was more than training. Let's just say I also learned something about building construction. I do not remember receiving pay for those training days. Still, I did not complain because that might have interfered with my becoming a police officer.

In my new uniform, I reported for roll call on the second floor at 22 West Broad Street, known as police headquarters. My platoon lieutenant appeared to be a mild-mannered man. My field sergeant assigned me to ride with the only Black police officer present that day.

He was big and burly with a mean disposition. He was well over two hundred and fifty pounds. I may have weighed one hundred sixty-five pounds wearing all of my equipment. I learned later I would not be assigned to ride with a White officer. Sure enough, when the other two Black officers were working, they rode together as partners. I was then assigned to walk Main Street, work in the radio room, or work at the front desk. I only rode in a police car when one of the other two Black officers was not working.

Our first stop on my first day was at a pool room on East Washington Street. Upon arrival, my partner entered first, and I followed. As soon as we entered, the very crowded room became eerily quiet. I followed my partner to the room's rear, scared and nervous. I'd played pool there many times. Would I be recognized? Finally, we left, and I exhaled.

As the evening continued and the skies grew darker, our pace increased. We were rolling from call to call, and most of the calls were fights of a domestic nature. This first day was a real learning experience because I had not yet attended the police academy. And, I had no idea when I would be attending. Finally, it was midnight; the shift ended. The drive back to

Laurens offered time for reflection. I commuted for six months before finally relocating to Greenville.

My assigned walking beat was on Main Street downtown. I took shelter in the police booth on Main and East Washington Streets on extremely cold or rainy days. It was a small green building with upper glass walls. Inside was a space heater and telephone, adequate for making phone calls and writing reports. Otherwise, I walked up and down the street, meeting people and checking on merchants. Three movie theaters were on Main Street, a couple of blocks apart: The Fox, The Carolina, and The Paris. Sometimes, I walked inside each theater, usually standing in the rear, scanning the crowd, and watching the movies for ten or fifteen minutes. Occasionally, I received a call to remove a rowdy or intoxicated person. The Paris Theater showed X-rated movies. The Carolina Theater showed mostly Black movies, like Shaft, Coffy, and Superfly. On the weekends, the entry lines were a block long. I enjoyed that assignment most of the time because of the positive social aspect.

Eventually, a couple of the younger White officers became a little friendlier toward me. Periodically as I walked my beat, one asked me to ride with him for a while. At times but not often, I was asked or directed to assist a White officer on a call. Usually, it would be at one of the rough downtown bars like "The Oasis" or "The Sanitary Cafe."

Within a few months, I was to report for two-week annual training with the National Guard. And in February, I reported to the police academy. When I returned to work after completing annual training, indirectly, a supervisor said I had to choose the National Guard or the police department. I resigned from the National Guard.

During the summer of that same year, there was an incident involving two White officers responding to a call in Fieldcrest Village. The residents were not happy with the way the officers responded. According to news reports, a crowd of about 300 gathered and yelled obscenities at the officers. Following the incident, a newspaper headline read, "Mayor Promises to Send Black Officer to Fieldcrest." The mayor said the community "will have its own black policeman by the end of the week." Only Black officers were to respond to calls in that area from that point on. In my opinion, that was the beginning of community policing for the Greenville Police Department.

True Stories of Over 100 Years…

Although on the job less than a year, I became that officer. I served as the community police officer in Fieldcrest Village for almost a year. My job description included becoming acquainted with the residents and liaison between the residents of the village and the police department. There were over three hundred units there, which equated to three hundred families. The children deserved much better. I started to enjoy my role of influence with the children in the village. The *Greenville News* captured and printed an image of me interacting with some of the kids.

Area patrolman builds rapport

Following a disturbance in Fieldcrest village last September, residents of the all-black community requested a community patrolman. Since the first of October, city police officer W. J. Harper has been working in that capacity.

His major duty, according to Lt. A. H. McKeown, administrative assistant to the chief of police, is to improve communications between the police and the residents.

"Through the community patrolman, we provide the citizens with a definite officer, a man they know personally who works in their community, whom they can contact if they have a problem," McKeown said.

Since his appointment, Harper has established a door-to-door campaign through which he has met more than half the Fieldcrest residents.

"About 85-90 per cent of the people I've met tell me they're glad I'm here and they'll work with me to make Fieldcrest a better place to live," Harper reported.

Despite his and residents' optimism, police say the crime rate for Fieldcrest, as for the rest of city, is on the increase.

During the first half of 1974, crimes committed in Fieldcrest included 1 murder, 2 rapes, 8 robberies, 30 housebreakings, 21 cases of larceny, 7 auto thefts and 24 assaults. This accounted for 2.79% of the crimes committed in the city during this time period.

While statistics covering the time since Harper has been assigned to Fieldcrest have not yet been compiled, residents feel things are quieter now.

However, McKeown explained, "Anytime you confine a large group of people to a small area, you have more potential for crisis situations."

(*Greenville News* Article about Harper as Community Officer)

True Stories of Over 100 Years...

(*Greenville News* Article about Harper as Community Officer)

Like most young officers, I too, in order to provide occasional necessities but mostly conveniences and creature comforts for my family, supplemented my income with outside part-time employment. At first, I worked security for department stores. I also worked in sales and delivery for Don Jones Stereo when VHS and Beta camcorders were first introduced. That was the start of another one of my small businesses, "Video Memories." I videotaped many weddings and special occasions for customers during that time. I also videotaped depositions for several attorneys. Most of those depositions were of victims who had been seriously injured by vehicle or an industrial accident or incident. It was necessary to get their testimony on file in case they died before the trial date.

As camcorders became more readily available and affordable for the general public, my video business declined. That is when I began a direct sales clothing business mainly for men. I sold the same brands as most department stores, but for much less. My focus was on men who wore suits every day, including attorneys, bankers, clergy, and yes, law enforcement. Johnson and Kelley claim to still have some of those suits.

True Stories of Over 100 Years…

Chief Johnson
Highlights, Challenges, & Accomplishments

True Stories of Over 100 Years…

True Stories of Over 100 Years…

Leadership has always been my forte. In Vietnam, I earned a Bronze Star and two other awards for combat valor. I hold many other awards, including the Strom Thurmond Award for Law Enforcement Excellence and the Billy Wilkins Court Award, so I believed applying for chief of police was well within my reach. When I entered law enforcement, there was no educational requirement for the chief of police position. However, when I applied for chief of police, the education requirement changed to a minimum of a bachelor's degree. I became the first African American chief of police in Greenville. For

African Americans, the requirements often change when we apply for certain jobs, so we have to be overprepared.

On August 3, 1970, a jailer named James Bagwell

was stabbed to death by an inmate trying to escape. I had been a rookie at the police department for less than a month. The suspect was unable to escape because a second jailer had closed a door and trapped him inside the jail. It was an extremely dangerous situation, but someone had to go in the jail and capture the inmate. As was the custom during this time, Black officers were often called for these assignments. My partner, Bobby Brown, and I were chosen, and this was one of the scariest times for me as a new officer. We went to an area called the "Bullpen" that had about fifty inmates, and my partner and I had about twenty-four rounds together. We subdued the inmate.

In 1975, I was assigned as a detective. A sheriff deputy, Lieutenant Frank Looper, and his father were shot and killed during a robbery. A suspect was developed as being responsible for the robbery and shooting of Looper. Again, Harold Jennings called me and told me that we needed to locate the guy. Within five or six hours, my partner and I found the suspect, Charles "Spanky" Wakefield, and arrested him on an outstanding warrant where he had beaten a family member. Once we arrested him, Jennings took us off that case and turned it over to two more senior officers.

Some people thought Wakefield was framed. However, I totally disagreed with those individuals.

In 1984, I graduated from the FBI National Academy. I was an honor graduate among 250 officers. I also graduated from the South Carolina Criminal Justice Academy and the American Baptist Theological Center, known as the Martin Webb Learning Center. Because of my close contact with Harold Jennings, I helped solve some of the biggest cases that occurred during that era.

**(Lieutenant Johnson Graduates
from FBI National Academy)**

Later in 1996, I was a major in the police department over investigations when an officer was killed. Being in charge of investigations, it was my responsibility to see that the guilty party was found, arrested, tried, and convicted. We had a lot of police officers with blood in their eyes because a fellow officer was killed. Locating Joe Shepard, the suspect, was difficult. As the head of investigations, I went to a council member and told her that we needed money to offer a reward for anyone willing to come forward with information. People begin to talk when money is involved. The council member spoke with the city manager, and we received reward money. We notified the community and within twenty-four hours, we knew where Joe Shepard was. Chief Jennings had taught me to call on the big play subordinates in special situations. Also, I learned early in my career from senior officers that it was important to have working relationships with the good, the bad and the ugly.

My career was not void of snares and traps from others who sought to spread negative rumors in efforts to derail my progress. There are three occasions I remember whereby fellow officers targeted me with entrapment on their minds.

The first incident took place after I was assigned to the metro narcotic unit. A waitress from a well-known bar in the area came to my office and offered to work undercover buying drugs for my partner and me. This offer made us suspicious, and we decided to check into it further. The waitress wanted to meet with me after hours, and she wore a very short mini dress, attempting to offer something that I had no interest in. Red flags went up, and I later learned that the bar she worked in was a spot where fellow law enforcement officers spent many hours. My thought at the time was why is she coming to me? Although I was single at the time, I could tell that this was nothing but a setup. I took a pass on any help from this "so-called informant."

On another occasion, a state constable came to my partner and me with a pound of marijuana, stating he wanted to turn it in. He said that his neighbor took it from his son and gave it to him for disposal. He "trusted" us, so he decided to give it to us to be destroyed. We took the marijuana and placed it in the city evidence locker. About a month later, my supervisor contacted me and stated that a complaint had been leveled against my partner and me. The complainant claimed to have turned in a pound of marijuana and we sold it on the street. I, along with my supervisor, went immediately to the evidence locker and the marijuana was still there. My supervisor stated he would report this incident to the head of the State Law Enforcement Division for Investigation. This was another attempted set up, and I remain unaware of the motivation behind it.

On a third occasion, a known alcoholic was arrested by uniform patrol officers. He had two hundred dollars in cash and heroin in his possession. This man had probably been arrested a hundred times for public drunkenness, but he was not known to sell or use drugs. My partner and I transported him to the jail and booked him on drug charges, placing his money and personal belongings with the desk sergeant. It was very apparent to my partner and me that someone was thinking we would take this man's money. Again, we were being tested and we did not know the source. Although we were officers of integrity and played by the rule of honesty, we were working with people who were attempting to destroy our careers and reputations.

On another occasion when I was head of investigations and we were working on a major case with the DEA (Drug Enforcement Administration), my boss received a call from another jurisdiction. The caller claimed I was working with a drug dealer who also ran a car lot. These were more lies and it required my boss to call in all the officers and set the record straight with them about who he knew me to be. This information is important to note because I want everyone to know the type of hostile work environment in which officers work. People will spread lies about your character and attempt to destroy your reputation out of sheer jealousy. In law enforcement, you must stay on your toes and watch your back at all times. What's unfortunate about these situations is that your coworkers should be trustworthy. Bitterness causes some to secretly dig holes for you and hate your guts. To sum this up, you can be stabbed in the back by people who work closely with you as well as those you know hate you. Race does not matter, because haters come in all colors. Therefore, my advice is to keep your nose clean and always do what is right. God has the last say and He will shine a light on your pathway. He did it for me.

When you are fulfilling your purpose, sometimes others will attempt to block your path. Therefore, you either drag them along or leave them behind. Pray that one day they wake up.

The department made a request through the federal protective service agencies that conducted the bomb canine dog training. We were put on the waiting list for training. However, there was a backlog list across the country that was two or three years long. Realizing that we could not wait because of the calls and requests we were receiving at the time, I decided to call on South Carolina's Senior United States Senator, Strom Thurmond.

I wrote a letter to the Late Senator Thurmond explaining the situation and that we were on a long waiting list. Lo' and behold, we received a call a week later from the canine training federal agency that someone had dropped off their list and the Greenville Police could have the slot. The police department identified the officer for the training, and we used drug seized assets to cover the cost for the canine unit. The rest is history!

True Stories of Over 100 Years…

(*Greenville News* Article on Chief Johnson)

Henry C. Harrison
1300 Rutherford Road
Greenville, S. C. 29609

Cheif,

I just read a letter from you to Strom Thurmond and allow me to say one of best compose letter that I have read. Jack Fengel, will never forget neither will I the confedence and trust you express to the Senator about him. I along with many other citizen feel safe having a Chief of your statue serving our

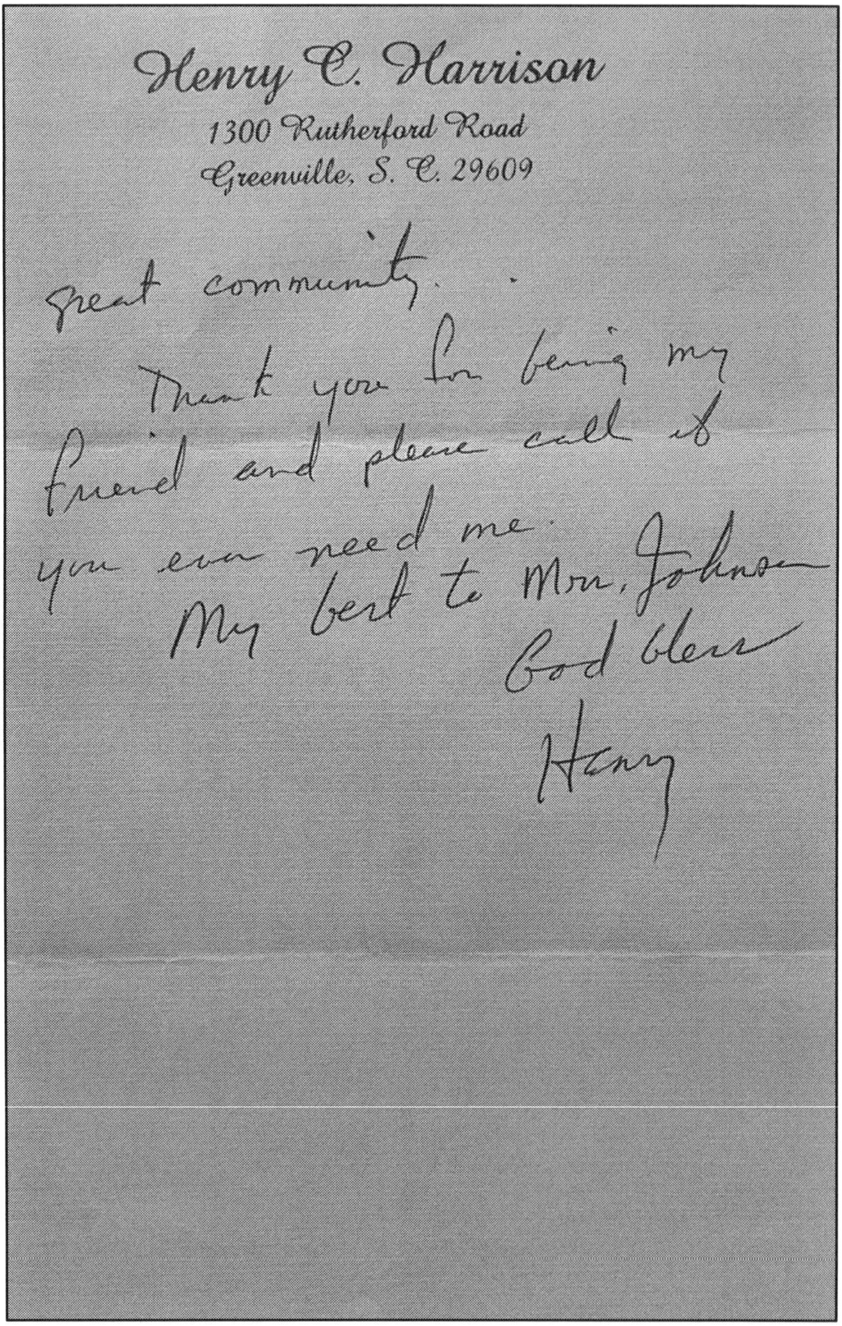

True Stories of Over 100 Years…

Henry C. Harrison
1300 Rutherford Road
Greenville, S. C. 29609

great community.
Thank you for being my friend and please call if you ever need me.
My best to Mrs. Johnson
God bless
Henry

True Stories of Over 100 Years...

(Johnson Pictured with Henry Harrison)

It is my desire to be remembered as the technology chief of police. When I was chief, we made changes in the Greenville Police Department, realizing that many of the problems we faced could be resolved using technology. For example, in 2000, we had numerous problems with teens doing gas drive-offs, stealing hubcaps, and other minor crimes. I, along with some of the other police chiefs in the state, met and suggested suspending the driver's licenses of the youth committing these crimes. After the law was passed supporting the suspension of licenses, these crimes dissipated. Generally, teenagers who have obtained their driver's licenses do not want anything interfering with their privilege of driving.

Downtown Greenville is an important place for the business community, so I suggested placing cameras throughout the area. As a result, over one hundred cameras were placed in downtown, and we were the first city in South Carolina to install cameras. The cameras made a profound improvement in crime prevention in the downtown district of Greenville. Some people were opposed at first, but now I think everyone loves the idea.

True Stories of Over 100 Years...

(*Greenville News* Article on Chief Johnson)

Today, as we know, there is a camera safety system at Haywood Mall. The consolidation of the police and fire dispatch centers was an important feat for me, as well. I was able to convert the police radio system to the Palmetto 800 Trunked System, which offered law enforcement the ability to intercommunicate. I was successful in securing take-home vehicles for all officers.

I started a Citizens Police Academy, which allowed

citizens to observe what police officers experience daily. The idea behind this was to have community leaders trained to advocate for officers in our absences.

During my administration, laptop computers were added to patrol cars. Because police officers were often involved in scuffles or fights with citizens and they sometimes came out on the short end of the stick, we purchased tasers for the officers. Tasers were the key component in ending the fights. This addition also decreased the workers' compensation claims filed within our department.

Through our involvement with Crime Stoppers, I wanted to encourage citizens to do their civic duty by reporting anyone involved in a crime in order to collect a reward. Twice, our department conducted a live crime most wanted show with local TV personality Liz Walker. During the show, people who were wanted by law enforcement were identified. Nationally known Reverend Jesse Jackson even assisted us by making a commercial asking citizens to turn in criminals. I was also responsible for implementing the Public Information Officer Association, a police museum, the department volunteer program, and the Enhanced

Crime Analysis Unit. These are some of the numerous upgrades and improvements made under my watch.

When asked the formula for my success at the Greenville Police Department, my response was that I knocked on the door at precisely the right time and was well qualified for the positions I held. A city council member stated in a local newspaper years ago "there was no tokenship involved in Johnson's advancement." I used my influence to grow other people who I felt would have my back; however, realistically that did not always work out. In life, you must think about others and keep a servant's heart. Surround yourself with team players, but always 'stay woke.' When you help others, they will help you.

When I retired as Chief of Police, the city proclaimed March 25-31, 2007, as "Chief Willie Johnson Week." I was also given a grand retirement party by the Greenville Community that was attended by over 1000 people.

True Stories of Over 100 Years…

CITY OF GREENVILLE   OFFICE OF THE MAYOR

Proclamation

WHEREAS, Chief Willie L. Johnson has served our country and community with honor, devotion and commitment; and

WHEREAS, Chief Johnson has been a positive influence in the growth and progress of Greenville; and

WHEREAS, Chief Johnson has been challenged daily in the performance of his duties, and he faced each challenge with integrity, fairness and compassion. His leadership and public service have earned him the respect and gratitude of people from all walks of life, not only in Greenville, but throughout the State of South Carolina.

NOW THEREFORE, I, Knox H. White, Mayor of the City of Greenville, South Carolina, do hereby declare the week of March 25 - March 31, 2007, as

CHIEF WILLIE L. JOHNSON WEEK

in the City of Greenville, and on behalf of City Council and the citizens of Greenville, we congratulate and thank Willie L. Johnson, retiring Chief of Police, City of Greenville, South Carolina for his dedicated career in law enforcement.

Signed, Sealed and Delivered this 20th day of March, 2007.

KNOX H. WHITE
Mayor

(Declaration from Mayor Knox White)

True Stories of Over 100 Years...

Awards

- Strom Thurmond Award for Excellence (1993) in Law Enforcement
- Jaycees' Officer of the Year
- Boy Scouts Silver Beaver Award
- Urban League Whitney M. Young Officer of the Year
- Rotary Officer of the Year
- Church & Community Service Award
- Church & Community Relations Award
- Order of The Palmetto State of SC
- Bell South Calendar Recognition Award
- Greenville Downtown Rotary Club Officer of the Year
- Judge Billy Wilkins Court Award
- Save Our Sons Board Member of the Year
- SHARE Community Services Award
- US Postal Service Commemorative Stamp Collection Recognition Award

True Stories of Over 100 Years...

Vietnam Awards

```
Vietnam Service Medal w/5 Bronze Service Stars; National Defense Service Medal;
Republic of Vietnam Campaign Medal; Combat Infantryman Badge; Air Medal;
Bronze Star Medal; Good Conduct Medal; Expert (Rifle);

USATC - Leadership Crs
USATC - NCO Combat Ldr Crs(Phase I)
USATC - NCO Combat Ldr Crs(PhaseII)
```

(Three Vietnam Awards and Training Captured from DD214)

- Bronze Star Medal (Meritorious Service in Combat & Star Award)
- Vietnam Service Medal
- National Defense Service Medal
- The Republic of Vietnam Campaign Medal
- Combat Infantry Badge
- Air Medal
- Good Conduct Medal
- Expert Rifle

True Stories of Over 100 Years...

Board Service

- State President of Palmetto State Law Enforcement Officers Association (PSLEOA)
- President for Greenville Police Pistol Club
- Save Our Sons (Vice President)
- Greenville Downtown Rotary Club
- Greenville Urban League of the Upstate
- The Phyllis Wheatley Association
- Boy Scouts of America Outreach Program (Vice President)
- YMCA
- American Legion
- VFW Post 6734
- Greenville Crime Stoppers
- Southeastern Crime Stoppers
- Greenville Braves
- COGNIS Chemical Corporation
- City of Mauldin Election Commission
- South Carolina Joint Terrorism Task Force
- Hillcrest Middle School Improvement Council
- Mauldin High School Improvement Council

True Stories of Over 100 Years…

True Stories of Over 100 Years...

Captain Kelley
Highlights, Challenges & Accomplishments

True Stories of Over 100 Years…

True Stories of Over 100 Years...

The experiences of Black officers at the Greenville City Police Department during my tenure were often cruel and insensitive. After Williams was elected Sheriff of Greenville County, I could not believe the difference in the two agencies. Even though I knew there were going to be situations similar to what I experienced at the City Police Department, I felt that conditions were improving in law enforcement as a result of Sheriff Williams offering me a job.

When I started with the Greenville County Sheriff's Office, I never worked as a uniformed officer as Sheriff Cash Williams promised me. I immediately began in the Vice and Narcotics Unit. There were only two Black officers in Vice and Narcotics, Harold Ross and me. My entire experience with the sheriff's office was different from the Greenville City Police Department in that there were fewer racial slurs used openly in the presence of Blacks.

One incident during my early years with the sheriff's office involved residents of Chanticleer, an affluent community in Greenville. The Chanticleer Community could be accessed from the Augusta Road and Pleasant Valley Community, a neighborhood composed mostly of Blacks who were less privileged. A meeting was held between the two communities to discuss the closing of the access road where Blacks residents could travel straight through Chanticleer. Sheriff Williams wanted to send some officers to ensure an orderly meeting. I was chosen as one of the officers to assist. I certainly had an interest as a current resident of the Pleasant Valley Community.

As expected, members of the Chanticleer Community started by giving reasons they wanted to close the bridge, such as the bridge was unsafe. The purpose of my presence was to keep order; however, after hearing the false rationale behind closing the road, I could not just sit there and be quiet. I said, "The reason you want this road closed is that you do not want Blacks coming through your community. If I get a call that there has been a break-in or some sort of illegal activity occurring in Chanticleer and the bridge is shut down and I live in that community, what do you expect me to do?"

The majority of my time spent at the sheriff's office was in the Vice and Narcotics Unit. I also had the opportunity to work in burglaries. Cash Williams was a four-year sheriff, lasting one term. Johnny Mack Brown succeeded Williams, and he asked me to continue my work at the sheriff's office. I told him if he'd have me, I would remain.

One of the most tragic moments for me was when my lieutenant, Frank Looper, a great investigator, was murdered, along with his father. I was one of his investigators and considered him a true friend. On January 31, 1975, Frank Looper and his father were gunned down at their residence in the West End District of Greenville. Frank died the next morning. The man charged with the murders, Charles Wakefield, spent thirty-five years in prison before he was released. From the day of his arrest until now, he has proclaimed his innocence. As a tribute to his dedication and legacy, the Frank Looper Award was founded in memory of Looper and is given annually to a deputy for outstanding work.

Simultaneously to Chief Willie Johnson working as city vice, I was working as county vice. We teamed together on a lot of cases. We both started working on drug cases before drugs were popular in Greenville. Willie Johnson, Harold Beeks, and I came up through the ranks together in vice and narcotics.

During my last six years at the Greenville County Sheriff's Office, I was promoted to Captain of Internal Affairs. That placed me in a somewhat unique position because our primary purpose was to investigate allegations against deputies. On the other hand, that position allowed me to ensure everyone was treated equally, whether the officer was White or Black. We made sure that procedures were above board. If someone was wrong, they were held accountable and in a lot of cases, officers lost their jobs.

Our department met with different community

groups and informed people that before we could act on any wrongdoing, someone had to file an official written complaint. If we knew officers were violating someone's rights or using discriminatory practices while carrying out their duties, we took it upon ourselves to initiate investigations.

After 29 years of service, I retired from the Greenville County Sheriff's Office on September 30, 1999. During my career, I gained the utmost respect for Sheriff Johnny Mack Brown for his management of the sheriff's office. He willingly addressed the concerns of all citizens in order to make Greenville County a better place. The respect he showed the other Black officers and me, that we had not experienced prior, is what made him stand out above the others. During my law enforcement career, I received many awards. Some of them include the Strom Thurmond Award for Excellence in Law Enforcement, the Billy Wilkins Award, and the Greenville City Rotary Award.

It was not long after retiring that I was asked by the chief of police at the Greenville-Spartanburg International Airport to work as an officer. This was shortly after the tragic events of 911. I accepted and served as a uniformed officer, working at the departure gate for about six or seven months. When the chief stated that he needed us to work ten-to-twelve-hour shifts, I knew it was time for me to go. I enjoyed meeting new people and working with the other officers, but I did not retire to return to work full-time.

Since then, I have used my time to do just what I want. I have always had a love for photography, so I, along with my friends Willie Harper, Charles Brock, and Stephon Lewers, started a photography group called Upstate Photographer's Guild. We currently have about thirty members. The camaraderie I have found with others who enjoy photography has been rewarding.

True Stories of Over 100 Years…

Captain Harper
Highlights, Challenges & Accomplishments

True Stories of Over 100 Years…

One of the primary reasons I wanted a career in law enforcement was that I thought it would be exciting to be a detective. Trying to solve an unknown was intriguing to me. I made detective in 1975. I served almost 30 of 33 years with the department in some investigative capacity. My detective partner was Willie Johnson, also from Laurens, who later became my boss as the chief of police. As detectives, we had some fascinating cases. I was Johnson's senior at Sanders High School, graduating a year before him. He was my senior by four years in the police department. Johnson taught me that a good detective must develop sources to be a successful investigator. Sometimes these sources are

(*Greenville News* Article about Harper's Promotion to Detective)

called "informants," "rats," or "snitches." Johnson had experience in working vice and narcotics drugs and, therefore, had developed plenty of sources! Our car was an unmarked white Ford. Unlike today, dress clothing was mandatory. The standard attire for detectives was a suit or jacket and necktie every day.

It was mandatory our firearms be concealed when in public. We were assigned cases ranging from petty theft to homicide. There were two shifts of detectives. The first shift was 0700-1500 hours, and second shift was 1500-2300 hours. Our working schedule was six days on and two days off. Johnson and I were detective partners for about a year until his promotion to sergeant in the Uniform Patrol Division.

Every police report case number ending in the number four was mine; Johnson's cases ended in the number seven. In our efforts to develop leads for our cases, sometimes it was necessary to look at the bigger picture and forgo a lesser crime. We needed supervisor approval if the case led us to another county or out of state. We were often paired with a Black SLED agent to travel out of state for extradition.

One of the first high-profile cases Johnson and I solved was the abduction and rape of two local university students. Two male subjects accosted the two victims as they were leaving a nightclub. They raped the female and pistol-whipped the male. Solving that case was gratifying, as these two were dangerous and responsible for crimes throughout the city and county.

As a detective, I once questioned a supervisor about my annual performance rating being lower than another detective whose case clearance rate was consistently lower than mine. He responded that the other detective, who had children to support, needed a larger salary. During this era, most Black police officers in the south can attest that a career in law enforcement was not a cakewalk. Throughout my career, I've had to tiptoe and navigate minefields of people with ill-intent, just because of my skin color.

Early in my career, although never directed at me, I witnessed White coworkers use the N-word in the workplace more than I care to remember. I seldom heard a White supervisor or manager using the N-word. Still, it wasn't unusual to hear White detectives use it in conversation with a White manager or supervisor. I never heard the superior correct or rebuke the subordinate. Therefore, in my view, the supervisor condoned that language, in effect, giving that person the okay to continue. There were times they did not care if I heard them, and sometimes I think they wanted me to hear them that I might react in a fashion that would lead to my termination. On several occasions, attempts were made to lure me into compromising situations to derail my career. The recurring question was: Do I succumb to the intimidation and get fired? Or do I stay and try to affect change from the inside? In addition, there were times I was directed to conduct unusual or dangerous assignments that could have easily led to injury or even death. I was considered "expendable," and to God be the glory that I survived.

There were many racial occurrences during my career. Once, I was conducting a follow-up on one of my cases, an HBGL (House Breaking & Grand Larceny) in the East North Street area. As usual, once a citizen called to report a crime, a uniformed officer responded by taking the report. A detective then interviewed the citizen to retrieve more information. This particular house had a screened-in front porch. I knocked on the door and the complainant, an older White lady, came out onto the porch. I explained our presence. She asked to see our badges, and we showed them to her. She went back into the house and then returned to the porch seconds later with a telephone to her ear. She had phoned the police department to tell them there were two "nigger men" at her door claiming to be detectives. Dispatch transferred her phone call to the detective division, where my supervisor verified our identity.

One afternoon while working, I received a call from my wife, who was pregnant with our first child. She said our house had been burglarized. I rushed home to find her hysterical. Someone had forced their way inside our home and badly damaged the front double doors. The thieves ransacked our home; items stolen included food, wine, clothes, gifts from family and friends for our firstborn, and other items. We lived in the Belle Meade section of Greenville County outside of the city limits, making it in the jurisdiction of the Greenville County Sheriff's Office. During this time in the seventies, house burglaries were a favorite activity for street criminals. My detective partner and I were alert for break-ins with the same modus operandi (M.O.). Weeks later, we arrested a man who had burglarized a house on McDaniel Avenue. After interviewing him, we found there were similarities to other unsolved break-ins. He was cooperative, and in a talkative mood, so we rode him around. My partner drove, while I sat in the back seat with our prisoner who pointed out other house break-ins he committed with his accomplices.

Finally, we drove to my neighborhood and asked if anything in that area was familiar to him. As we passed my house, the burglar said, "Oh, yes! That house with the red double doors. We broke into that house…" while naming his accomplices. He confessed to taking food, clothing, and wine and playing pool. He said they left in a hurry after finding a police uniform in one of the closets. From that initial arrest on McDaniel Avenue, we cleared many more burglaries. The young man and his three or four accomplices all pled guilty in court, which resulted in a court sentence and an order to pay restitution to the victims.

All in all, my years as a detective were engaging and fulfilling. I had a couple of embarrassing events, such as losing my handcuffs. During a search for stolen goods in Fieldcrest Village, the person on the arrest warrant was hiding behind a pile of clothing. Another officer and I managed to handcuff the struggling lady. We continued searching for evidence while she ran out of the front door, never to be seen again, at least by me. Of course, I was the subject of jokes by fellow officers for longer than I want to remember. I heard my cuffs were in the state of New Jersey more than once.

Another embarrassing event involved the case of a missing woman, which her husband reported. His reactions and story raised some suspicions. We didn't have any promising leads, so we paid him an unannounced home visit. Like before, during the interview, his answers to our questions were inconsistent, which heightened our suspicion of him. We asked if we could look around; he consented. In one of the rooms was a conspicuous area where a large oval rug had been. A closer examination of the floor revealed what appeared to be bloodstains. The husband did not incriminate himself at that time, and we didn't have probable cause to arrest him. He agreed to take a polygraph examination and passed it.

Days later, the complainant appeared at the police department and confessed. He gave a detailed account of killing his wife, wrapping her in the oval rug, and dumping her in the city landfill. We requested assistance from the grounds and sanitation department and prepared to search the landfill. We didn't find a body that day, but on another day, the missing wife showed up at the station to report she wasn't dead. Do I need to say anything else?

I became a detective sergeant in 1978. Because there was no increase in salary, I approached my captain regarding this. He referred me to the human resources director. The HR director attempted to explain why my promotion did not warrant an increase, which just didn't make sense to me. When I asked for an appointment with the city manager, the HR director's position changed.

(*Greenville News* Article Announcing Harper's Promotion to Detective Sergeant in 1978)

I supervised a five-person detective squad and two juvenile detectives. During that era, female officers generally served as juvenile detectives. In death investigations, detectives often attended autopsies. I never liked viewing autopsies, but there was one detective on my squad who seemed thrilled to participate in autopsies. I was the sergeant, so I delegated, which solved that problem.

Needless to say, as the first young Black detective supervisor, I faced challenges almost daily. My entire squad was White, and most were older than me. Within the first few months, two of them were insubordinate, blatantly refusing to do what I asked. I had no choice but to report their behavior to my superiors, who fully supported me.

One morning around 3 AM, dispatch awakened me and said I needed to come in. Uniformed patrol officers were at the scene of a burning vehicle near Church Street and University Ridge. Ordinarily, I would not have received a call about a burning car, but this car had a partially burned dead body in the trunk. The result was an insurance fraud and murder case, a scheme that quickly fell apart when the fire did not completely burn the body and contents. We developed a lead to High Point, NC, and I called for a detective to accompany me. Arriving an hour before sunrise, we met with the High Point police and devised a plan before making an arrest. Working all night and the next day, we transported the male suspect back to

Greenville. The suspect and his female accomplice confessed their criminal strategy to collect on a life insurance policy of the male suspect. First, they drove through the streets of Atlanta, searching to find someone that fit the physical description of the insured. The suspects had snatched the unassuming victim from the streets of Atlanta, taken him to a motel room, shot him, and slashed his throat. Then they put the clothing and identification on the victim's dead body and drove it to Greenville before setting him on fire. After lengthy investigations in High Point, Greenville, and Atlanta, all defendants pled guilty to murder.

True Stories of Over 100 Years…

FULTON COUNTY

LEWIS R. SLATON
DISTRICT ATTORNEY-ATLANTA JUDICIAL CIRCUIT
THIRD FLOOR COURTHOUSE • ATLANTA, GEORGIA 30335

December 5, 1983

Chief of Police
Greenville Police Department
4 McGee Street
Greenville, S. C. 29601

Re: State of Georgia vs.
Ronald Gaither, Roosevelt
McRae, Karen McRae

Dear Sir:

    I want to commend Detectives Heyward Davis, W. Harper and Officer J. Burgess for their outstanding service in connection with the above murder case. Because of the fine job they did these defendants had no choice but to plead guilty. Ronald Gaither received a sentence of Life and twenty years to serve. Roosevelt McRae received a sentence of Life and Karen McRae received a sentence of ten years to serve.

    The conduct of these officers is in the highest tradition of law enforcement and they should be commended.

    Thank you for your cooperation.

Sincerely,

A. Thomas Jones
Assistant District Attorney
Atlanta Judicial Circuit

**(Letter of Commendation from
Fulton County District Attorney Office)**

Another high-profile case began one spring weekend when I was on duty. A couple entered my office, and the man reported his mother missing. His mother had recently remarried and had never gone very long without communicating with her son. The interview of the husband did not produce any helpful information. He stated he did not know his wife's whereabouts, that she had left him a couple of weeks prior. The investigation continued into the missing woman's whereabouts for the next several weeks. Each of my interviews with the husband yielded a different story. I received a break in the case when the missing woman's credit card was used, and we found an existing court warrant on the husband.

After his arrest on the court warrant, the husband continued to give conflicting stories. The Director of the Greenville County Crime Lab and I searched his residence. Not finding any evidence of substance inside, we donned our coveralls and crawled underneath the house. If someone were to bury something under the house, the most probable place would be at the highest point. So, we started at that location, noticing an area of disturbed ground. Using a shovel, I started digging gently in the area of disrupted earth. Ten minutes of careful digging passed, then the shovel struck something hard. The most pungent odor of decomposition arose from the ground. The digging continued until we were sure it was a body. I stopped, and the crime lab personnel continued digging while I documented the unearthing of the body. When it was confirmed to be the missing wife's body, my next step was to interrogate the husband. I wouldn't have to look for him this time. Once back at headquarters, my interview with the husband commenced once I advised him of Miranda rights. He adamantly denied knowing his wife's whereabouts or what happened to her. That is until I presented information known only to the killer. With this, he broke. The autopsy indicated his wife died by strangulation. He was convicted of murder and sentenced to life in prison, where he died at age forty-seven.

True Stories of Over 100 Years...

Man charged with wife's murder

A Greenville man was arrested Thursday for the slaying of his wife, who had been reported missing for approximately the pass six weeks.

Ronald Eugene Amrine, 43, of 300 Stewart St., was charged with murder and was being held at the Greenville County Detention Center. Bond was not set.

The partially decomposed body of his wife, Mary P. Amrine, 54, was discovered by Greenville city detectives at approximately 11:30 a.m. Thursday in a grave beneath the house.

Mrs. Amrine was reported missing March 30 by her son-in-law, who told police that he had been unable to contact her since late February.

Upon receiving the report, city detectives promptly approached Amrine. He told them his wife had left him in mid-March and he was uncertain of her whereabouts.

"We suspected that some foul play was involved," said Capt. Earl Barnett. "So we kept going with the thing."

After an investigation, detectives concluded that Amrine's initial statement was in conflict with those made by neighbors and the woman's relatives.

Detectives returned to the Amrine resident Thursday and found the body. Amrine was arrested a few hours later.

Detectives were uncertain of when Mrs. Amrine died.

Greenville County Corner Stan McKinney said an autopsy was performed Thursday afternoon on the victim by a pathologist at Greenville General Hospital, who determined the cause of death as ligature strangulation.

"We had suspected that was the cause," McKinney said. "A piece of clothing was used" in the incident.

(*Greenville News* Article about Murder Investigation)

Approximately eighteen months later, I was selected as the first Black officer from the Greenville Police Department to attend the FBI National Academy (FBINA) in Quantico, Virginia. Although it was difficult for her, my wife Winnie fully supported me. I was gone for eleven weeks, only returning for monthly weekend visits. Winnie attended to our four-year-old daughter Andrea and nine-month-old son Jamie alone while holding down a full-time job.

My class, the 128th Session of the FBI-NA, represented 250 law enforcement officers from 49 states, including DC, Puerto Rico, the Virgin Islands, Canada, Egypt, England, Indonesia, Taiwan, Zimbabwe, and all branches of the military. The SCCJA was intense, but it was a breeze compared to the FBI Academy. Of all the excellent law enforcement trainings I had received up to this point, the FBI-NA was the pinnacle. I did well in all facets of the academy. I placed near the top of the two hundred fifty students in the firearm competition. And, by the way, in the single-elimination pool tournament, I was named the FBI-NA 128th Session Pool Champion.

Finally, it was graduation day. I was delighted, especially with Winnie and Andrea there, to witness this occasion. In addition to graduation day, Andrea met her grandfather for the first time.

Many friendships developed from this academy class, and this new fraternity tremendously enhanced my career. If I needed assistance on an investigation from another state, I called an FBI-NA graduate who was always ready and willing to help.

My promotion to lieutenant in 1987 was to the Uniform Patrol Division as a platoon lieutenant. On May 24, 1989, I was in my office completing paperwork when I heard a broadcast over the radio of a barricaded suspect with a gun. I immediately dropped my work and headed to the scene on Randall Street. A shotgun blast rang out from the house soon after I arrived. At the same time, an officer grabbed his face while falling to the ground. He was in an open area; I directed a patrol car to the site to provide cover for the wounded officer while he was being attended. Although he was shot in the face with a shotgun, the excellent news was that his wounds were not life-threatening, and he eventually returned to work. After the approximately three-hour standoff, officers stormed the house and arrested the suspect without anyone being seriously injured. I was proud of our officers' responses and how they conducted themselves.

After the May 24 event, *The Greenville News* headline read, "Police officers lauded for handling face-off." As expected, this event received extensive news coverage. One of the television news channels aired the event several times per day for days showing me using a tree for cover.

Police officers lauded for handling of face-off

Officer recovering from shotgun wounds

By Bob Piazza
News staff writer

Greenville police officials Wednesday commended the officers involved in Tuesday's dramatic three-hour standoff at a downtown duplex, during which a police officer suffered head and leg wounds from a shotgun blast.

"If it happened again today, I would hope they would act just exactly the same way," Chief Mike Bridges said. "I have not found any fault with the operation whatsoever."

Bridges said his department would review the incident in the hope that officers might learn something helpful for future situations, but he was "very pleased" with the department's performance.

Officer Steven Sipe, 34, of Taylors, was shot in the lip, face, head and leg, but he was treated and released from Greenville Memorial Hospital several hours after the shooting, officials said. Sipe, a seven-year veteran of the department, was resting at home Wednesday, Bridges said.

The standoff began around 5:15 p.m. Tuesday on Randall Street near North Main Street when Sipe and another officer tried to serve papers on Willie Atkins Jr. ordering a psychiatric examination, Capt. Earl Watson said.

Atkins, who was described by relatives and authorities as having suffered from psychiatric problems for several years, barricaded himself in his home and then later fired on the officers, officials said.

The court papers served on Atkins, 31, of 107 Randall St., alleged that he had not been taking his medication lately, said Lt. W.J. Harper.

Harper said Atkins was taken to a psychiatric hospital in Columbia Tuesday night, after authorities rushed his house and disarmed him.

Atkins was charged with assault and battery with intent to kill, resisting arrest with a deadly weapon and malicious damage to private property, according to warrants.

Bridges said the court-issued papers were part of an involuntary commitment procedure that begins at the county probate judge's office.

County Probate Judge Ralph Drake said he was prevented by state confidentiality laws from commenting on Atkins' case, but that the next step in an involuntary commitment procedure would involve an examination by a doctor at a mental health center.

If the doctor finds a person mentally ill and dangerous, the person would then be committed to a state psychiatric hospital, Drake said.

Bridges said his officers serve about 200 orders for psychiatric evaluations a year, and the procedure followed in serving the papers won't be altered.

During the three-hour standoff officers fired about a dozen tear gas canisters into Atkins' house and one officer discharged his weapon during the confrontation Watson said.

Harper declined to identify the officer Wednesday but said police officials would review the action taken by the officer.

(*Greenville News* Article about Wounded Police Officer)

Some of my friends, especially a deacon at my church, constantly made me the brunt of jokes about the tv news clip. The deacon said I was hiding behind a tree, embellishing his story even more when in the presence of other church members. For a while after that, if I saw him before he saw me, he wouldn't see me.

Occasionally, as a platoon lieutenant, I was called upon to conduct internal investigations and other functions of the Internal Affairs Division. Of all of my assignments, one of the more challenging and rewarding assignments was recruiting Black officers. My frequent frustration centered around the apparent racism I experienced while on that assignment. It was evident that a few White city government employees did not support this assignment. Some city council members were concerned about the lack of diversity in the police department, specifically Black officers. One top police official did not view diversity as a priority. His defense was that Black officers were difficult to recruit. One of the Black council members asked if the department had tried assigning and using Black officers to recruit Black candidates. His answer was "no." As a result, Chief Harold Jennings sent me on the road to recruit. He gave me a car and the latitude to handle the logistics; he only wanted results.

Immediately, I reflected on my days of recruiting for the National Guard. I started to question myself. How can I make this assignment successful? The recruiting and background investigations were under the Internal Affairs Division of the police department. Therefore, I reported directly to the Internal Affairs Commander, who showed me his strategies. Our approaches to this assignment were not even close.

Computers with the Disk Operating System (DOS) debuted shortly before this time, but no computers were in the Internal Affairs Division. Stored handwritten files and documents were in a bound accounting ledger. I acquired a desktop computer, loaded it with the spreadsheet software Lotus 123, word processing software WordPerfect, and database software dBase. I sought every computer workshop and class available to learn these programs to make my job more manageable. I didn't become a whiz in computers, but compared to my superiors, I became proficient.

The first place I recruited was in my hometown of Laurens. I drove to the Laurens Police Department, met with the chief, and explained my assignment. I asked if he knew of any Black applicants for whom he did not have openings. He pulled a few applications and gave me the name of Rodney Neely and a couple others. Over the next two or three weeks, I repeated this process at police departments in Greenwood, Spartanburg, and other cities throughout the state. I visited the Military Police Army Reserve and National Guard Centers. The staff members were supportive by providing rosters of soon-to-be ETS (expiration term of service) soldiers that included all of the information for contacting the potential officers. In addition, I met with the Greenville Ministerial Alliance, requesting them to announce to their congregations that the Greenville Police Department was hiring.

With an adequate pool of names, I contacted the prospects to gauge their level of interest. Candidates underwent background investigations before being hired that included education, criminal and credit histories, and unannounced home visits. Additionally, we interviewed the applicant's high school teachers and sometimes principals. Finalists underwent physical, psychological, and medical exams and an interview by the Civil Service Commission. It was disappointing to learn some people within the city's organization were working against my assignment and these candidates. It is not my intention to paint the organization with a broad brush. Let me be clear. Only two or three people I am aware of shared in these schemes that presented obstacles in hiring Black police officers. But those two or three people were in critical positions to derail applicants from advancing in the hiring processes. And sometimes, that is all it takes to thwart an operation. In several instances, once a candidate made it to the medical examination, I was informed the candidate had failed. He was "eaten up with diabetes," "had a heart problem," or another debilitating disease that the candidate was unaware of. Most of these candidates were adamant the medical results were in error and therefore requested a second doctor's opinion with more favorable results.

Approximately six months later, seven or eight candidates had completed all phases of the hiring process. Chief Jennings seemed pleased, and he proudly presented the candidates at a city council meeting. Some of the first in that group of Black officers continued on to successful careers. Rodney Neely was one of those candidates. Within a few years, he was promoted to a community patrol officer and later to detective. After about ten years in law enforcement, he started his own private investigative and security company. One of the goals of my assignment was for the police department to reflect the diverse community it serves. For the remainder of my career, I was responsible for recruiting, hiring, and managing those processes.

As a lieutenant affiliated with Internal Affairs, it was convenient for superiors to assign me to investigate misconduct allegations against police employees. In the early nineties, a police officer was accused of mishandling a fourteen-year-old Black male, a case I was assigned to investigate. One of the specific allegations against the officer was excessive force. This case, dubbed the "Hampton Street Bridge Incident," received extensive media attention. As a result of the findings, the officer lost his job for failing to follow procedures. Several other officers received lesser disciplinary actions for their roles in this incident.

In my thirty-three years in law enforcement, with almost thirty years conducting investigations, I have found that two critical components for solving the unknown are interviewing and interrogation. There is a difference between the two. As a young detective, I

True Stories of Over 100 Years...

took courses in Kinesics Interview Techniques, which involved evaluating what the interviewee said compared to their nonverbal communication and body language. It is very effective. I find myself using the Kinesic Interview practice in my everyday life when interacting with people.

(Greenville News Article about Harper's Promotion to Division Commander)

When the Internal Affairs Commander retired, I inherited the division and title of commander. I was now a member of the command staff. However, something was missing. I did not receive a salary increase nor the rank of captain that the other four division commanders held. Every other division commander before this time was a captain. Two other lieutenants were promoted to captain, although my tenure and qualifications exceeded one. Each division commander was required to attend the chief of police's daily command staff meetings to discuss the business of our divisions and the department's general operational strategies.

During subsequent annual performance appraisals, I requested a promotion to captain. Although I consistently received exemplary reviews, I was never given, in my opinion, a credible response for not being promoted. I knew the underlying reason, so I consulted with an attorney and seriously considered filing a complaint with the EEOC. I also considered just leaving the department, neither of which I did.

After commanding the division as a lieutenant for about seven years, in January of 1998, Chief Bridges promoted me to captain. With the promotion came additional responsibilities. I assumed the duties of accreditation manager for the department. A few years earlier, the internal affairs division, later renamed the Professional Standards Division, earned national accreditation status with the Commission on Accreditation for Law Enforcement Agencies (CALEA). Managing this program and process was a major challenge. Through the drafting and implementation of policies and standards, or "general orders," my goal was to improve the experiences of anyone that encountered a Greenville Police officer. The position of accreditation manager provided the opportunity to affect change within the department. For example, one of the most common complaints from motorists, especially people of color, was that they often felt racially profiled. In other words, in their opinion, officers had no lawful reason to stop them. Let us not kid ourselves; we know that happens. I drafted a general order that mitigated profiling during police traffic stops. The command staff eventually approved it, but not without difficulty, which was often the case. As a minority, introducing these types of changes to the command staff wasn't easy. I encountered recurring challenges by introducing what some considered to be controversial policies that required a majority vote to approve. Many of the officers didn't like the idea of CALEA and the changes it brought, but they had to accept them. And now, one of my responsibilities was to enforce inheritance.

Other significant objectives were to create a more diverse workforce within the police department and hold officers accountable for their actions. If officers know internal investigations will be conducted fairly and they will be held responsible for their actions, their conduct will improve.

CALEA is a credentialing authority through the joint efforts of law enforcement's major executive associations. Those associations are as follows:

- International Association Chiefs of Police (IACP)
- National Association of Black Law Enforcement Executives (NOBLE)
- National Sheriffs Association (NSA)
- Police Executive Forum (PERF).

Once earning initial CALEA accreditation, an accredited law enforcement agency must withstand a rigorous successful inspection every three years to achieve reaccreditation. Our department had more than three hundred standards or general orders to adhere to and enforce. As the Professional Standards Division Commander, I was responsible for departmental functions such as accreditation, recruitment, the Promotion Assessment Program, safety, internal affairs, victim services, CAPAR (crime analysis planning and research), property and evidence, supply, and the department's website. In addition, another responsibility was to monitor all of the department's computer contents.

On the first of each month, I received a printout from the city's IT (information technology) listing all the prohibited websites visited. The abuses were mostly shopping, music streaming, and occasionally a porn site visit. Internal investigations and complaints varied from one end of the spectrum to the other. Most complaints from the public were of rudeness and excessive force. And on occasion, a complaint from an officer's significant other regarding a domestic squabble surfaced. For example, a female police officer's spouse complained they had a spat, and the officer hid his complete set of dentures and wouldn't return them. Another more serious investigation involved the allegation of an officer's improperly handling more than fifty thousand dollars. Needless to say, I was not the most popular police employee. And yes, I did receive some threats throughout my career, most of which were by telephone.

Shortly after being promoted to captain and assuming these responsibilities, I became a CALEA national assessor, which required some travel to assess other law enforcement agencies. Of all the assessments I was charged with, those conducted in the San Francisco area and a sheriff's department near Chicago are most memorable. I suppose because they were my first and last assessments.

In early 1999, rumors began flowing that Chief Bridges was considering retiring due to health concerns. If he retired, most of us thought Johnson, a major and the second highest ranking officer, would become chief. And, combining tenure and rank, I was next in line. In the past, the appointment to chief by the Civil Service Commission came from within the ranks of the police department. They would select the next chief per the Civil Service Commission rules as I read them. I never aspired to serve as chief, but I wanted the promotion to major if Johnson were selected.

A *Greenville News* article was published in the Spring of 1999 titled "Greenville may abolish panel on civil service." The handwriting was on the wall. According to one *Greenville News* article, "some city officials had speculated a national search for police chief was a good idea." Were city officials attempting to change the procedures? Why? Again, I think most of us know the answer. Two loyal and dedicated officers (who happened to be Black) had worked their way up through the ranks to command and management levels. By the long-established rules, the major was eligible for the top position. Now, someone wanted to change the long-standing practice. The rules did not change, at least not this time. The headlines read, "Rule handcuffs search for Greenville Police Chief." Johnson was promoted to chief of police. As I stated earlier, I thought this was my opportunity for promotion to major. A year or so later during my annual performance appraisal, I expressed my interest in being promoted, only to be told a council member did not think it was a good idea for the two top positions in the department to be held by minorities. Was that ever a concern in previous administrations when two White people were at the helm of a city department? Will that be a concern to council members in future administrations when two Whites are the top two of a city department? Is it a city council concern right now where the top two people in that department are White? I'm just asking. In 2007, I retired as a captain.

On three occasions as a detective, I faced situations where I had to wrestle a gun from a subject, once by myself. The other two times, it was with the help of a fellow officer. In my 33-year career, I consider it a blessing never to have fired my weapon at a human. However, I did pull and point my service weapon about a half dozen times, but I thank God I never had to fire it other than in training. And I do believe during those occurrences of pointing my gun if I had fired it, it would have been a justifiable shooting. I like to think the vast majority of the officers I worked with had no desire to fire their weapons at another human being. However, I will admit, a few officers gloated at the opportunity. For example, one SWAT team member seemed proud to wear a shirt with the writing, "Happiness is a green light."

My wife Winnie and children have been a significant influence on my life. Winnie and I were married in 1974, six months after I joined the city police department. Winnie was a freshman in high school when I met her, and I was a senior. The first time I saw her, I liked what I saw. She had a cute and unforgettable smile. During my senior year, we talked often. After graduating and joining the military, we did not see each other, nor did we communicate for a while. I received a letter from her after about eighteen months in the army. When I was in Germany, we wrote to each other consistently until I was discharged and returned home. We started dating, and five years later, we were married. Our first child, a beautiful daughter, was born in 1978, and three years later, a handsome son was born. Fond memories of my children as young kids will forever linger. My daughter now resides in Atlanta, Georgia, and my son lives in Columbia, South Carolina.

Since my retirement, outdoor photography has been my passion. My love for scenic photography and long road trips has allowed me to drive through forty states and photograph and hike in most of them. I have also visited national parks, rainforests in the Caribbean, and Puerto Rico.

I am very blessed to have some of my fine art photography to have been on display and sold from art galleries in Greenville, Laurens, and Aiken Counties. I'm equally blessed to have my photography on the walls of manufacturers, hospitals, physicians, and business offices.

True Stories of Over 100 Years…

True Stories of Over 100 Years…

Chief Johnson
Advice to Current & Future Officers

True Stories of Over 100 Years…

True Stories of Over 100 Years...

- If you want to be involved in law enforcement, there will be challenges that you will face. But choose your fight. Do not fight everything and everybody. Choose your battles carefully.
- Do not stress out. Control what you can control. Some things will simply be out of your control. Some things will be above your pay grade.
- Do not owe people. Let people owe you. In other words, if somebody asks you to do something, do it. If somebody needs help, help them if you

can. This attitude worked out great for me in my career. You should be kind to everyone because you never know where help is going to come from later. For example, I worked a record hop for a lady named Ruby Jones on Saturdays when I was an officer. She paid ten dollars for security. Several times after working the night, Mrs. Jones told me she did not make any money so she could not pay me. She said to me, "Officer Johnson, you are going to need help from somebody one day, so you call on me and I will be there." Later in life when I was seeking a promotion, Mrs. Jones was a voice for me.

- Learning where the real power lies in the community is mandatory. Some folks just make noise.
- You must know how to bridle your tongue. Do not get mad about everything and display your anger. Controlled fury is important.
- Do not be a constant complainer.
- Do not fall into the trap of talking negatively with other officers at the water fountain. Oftentimes, when people fall into those traps, the people listening will report what you said, causing you

to have enemies you do not even know you have. You can listen but until you earn your place, do not participate. Take time and earn your place in the organization for which you work.
- Communication skills are extremely important. You have to know how to talk to people correctly and not talk down to them.
- Take advantage of every training opportunity that comes your way.
- Find a mentor inside and outside the agency. I was fortunate that when I came along, my mentor was a captain inside the police department who later became chief of police. His name was Harold Jennings. When I worked for him, I made him look good and he did not forget me. You want to choose a mentor who pulls you up the ladder with him. That is exactly what Harold Jennings did for me.
- Education is a must if you want to move up the ladder.
- Stay physically fit in order to offer your best service in law enforcement.
- Have tough skin and know that you represent

the people who came before you.
- Be willing to step outside of your comfort zone and take assignments that will expose you and others to greater opportunities. This will make you a stronger and better leader.
- As a former police chief, I recommend that you have what I call a "go-to-person." This is someone you can call on and know they will get the job done. I share this because a former supervisor had three people he always called on and we came through. If it was a sports team, I would say have "big play" officers.
- Making a living while making a difference at the same time is a worthy sacrifice.
- Do not "dumb-it-down" to be accepted in certain groups. It is not their fault if they don't know the real you. It's your fault for giving them a watered-down version of you.
- Sheriffs run for their jobs *every four years*. Police chiefs run for their job *every day*.

True Stories of Over 100 Years…

Captain Kelley

Advice to Current & Future Officers

True Stories of Over 100 Years…

True Stories of Over 100 Years…

Anyone desiring to enter law enforcement must have it in their heart. It is a job where the pay does not compensate for the danger you are exposed to on a daily basis or the countless hours you miss away from your family. I entered law enforcement because I wanted to help as many people as I possibly could. It was not about incarcerating people but helping individuals who committed crimes to find another path in life. There have been moments when people I encountered early in my career have approached me and thanked me for taking the time to talk with or listen to them. It kept them from making some bad decisions and going down the wrong path. Sometimes, it's just that simple. You cannot help everyone, but I felt as long as I offered help, it was up to the individuals to make the change.

Recently, Chief Willie Johnson, Captain Willie Harper, and I met with a large number of African Americans who are currently in law enforcement during the PSLEOA, Palmetto State Law Enforcement Officer Association, meeting. The majority of the officers did not know us. But after we gave them insight into what we experienced in law enforcement, they felt encouraged that they now have someone to lean on if they have problems.

It was really disheartening to see that the progress we thought we made seemed to be sliding backwards. When I look at the number of **African Americans and other underrepresented minorities in law enforcement who hold supervisory roles**, I am discouraged. We are not only underrepresented in law enforcement but at fire departments and emergency management services as well. It goes without saying that more African Americans and minorities are needed in law enforcement. The visual presence of minorities adds more accountability and assurance to the community. Part of the solution for the discord today is hiring more qualified African Americans and minorities in positions where they can make a difference as officers, supervisors, and recruiters.

True Stories of Over 100 Years…

True Stories of Over 100 Years…

Captain Harper
Advice to Current & Future Officers

True Stories of Over 100 Years…

- Do not go into law enforcement for reasons other than a genuine willingness to serve humanity.
- Law enforcement is not easy and is often a thankless occupation.
- If you are dealing with a male, regardless of the reason, treat him as if he is your father, husband, or brother. If it is a female, treat her as if she is your mother, wife, or sister.

- Choose your battles; you cannot win them all. What is the point in winning the battle and losing the war?
- We all know the difference between right and wrong. Do what is right.
- As a law enforcement officer, you will be challenged, and you will be tempted. And just to be real, that increases several times over if you are Black.
- There is never a right way to do something wrong.
- Do not become quickly discouraged.
- If law enforcement is truly your calling, the chances are good that you will have a rewarding career.

True Stories of Over 100 Years…

Chief Johnson
If You See Something Say Something

True Stories of Over 100 Years…

True Stories of Over 100 Years...

In closing, there are many great officers in the profession of law enforcement and that includes city, county, state, and federal. However, they have been dishonored by the bad law enforcement officers in the profession. Retired bad officers on Facebook encourage other bad officers, which is unfortunate.

To the current officers on the front line, support each other, and speak out to rid your agency of the people who are tarnishing the badge. If current law enforcement leaders will not listen, contact someone who is trusted within your community and let them speak up for you. Choose somebody with rapport and respect who can be trusted, such as an elected official, a private citizen, or the FBI. Your actions can save law enforcement.

Also, most agencies claim to be accredited and have written policies and procedures that they adhere to. Community leaders need to request a copy of the procedures and be prepared to file a written complaint when they feel they have been wronged. Make complaints about these bad officers so they can be weeded out. At the same time, when you witness an officer doing something well, make the officer's agency aware of it. Report the good along with the bad. Independent organizations from the federal level outside the state where the incident occurred should investigate all fatal shooting incidents and choose investigating units who are trained for these cases.

Currently, some departments cannot or will not police themselves. The police have lost the trust of many people in the communities they serve. I acknowledge that enough is enough, and I am sure you know all shootings are not justified. There is also social media where you can post information that you know to be true. Wrong is wrong and right is right. Call out those bad apples; they must be held accountable here and now. Also, know that God will have the last word.

True Stories of Over 100 Years…

Captain Harper
<u>*If You See Something Say Something*</u>

True Stories of Over 100 Years...

I believe this slogan, "If You See Something Say Something," was coined following the 9-11 attack on New York in 2001. Today, that phrase is befitting because of law enforcement's atrocious acts to persons of color across the country. Any and everyone should say something if a human is treated inhumanely. I have seen something in the past few years, so I am saying something. Defund the police? If that is what it sounds like, that is ridiculous. "Who ya gonna call?" More sensible measures should be taken, such as practical police reform and judicial reform. If we are to have a judicial system that truly administers justice, I said *justice*; there must be transparency and accountability throughout all components and elements of the judicial system. Remember Breonna Taylor who Louisville Metro Police officers killed in her apartment? To date, no one has been held accountable for her wrongful death. I believe that is in part because of the grand jury system. The system is better served if grand juries hear the whole story from the prosecution and the defense.

According to national news articles, there are many similar cases of system abuse. Examples include the Ahmaud Arbery case in Georgia; the murder of Laquan McDonald, shot 16 times by Chicago police officer Jason Van Dyke who was charged and convicted, only after a judge, against police desires, released the videotape of the shooting. In another case, a neighborhood about a mile from my residence, a Greenville County Deputy reportedly shot a resident through the front door of his home. According to news reports, locally and nationally, the deputy reported the resident opened the door and fired at the deputy first. Days later, the body cam indicated that did not happen. Similar incidents are occurring all too frequently. Police supervisors know who these problem officers are. It is time for them to man or woman up against the indignities, injustices, and sometimes criminal acts committed by officers under their command. So yes, I think this country is overdue for police and judicial reform, NOT DEFUNDING.

True Stories of Over 100 Years…

True Stories of Over 100 Years...

Chief Johnson's
Photos and Memorabilia

True Stories of Over 100 Years…

True Stories of Over 100 Years…

(Detective Willie Johnson Providing Security for Miss America, Vanessa Williams, 1983)

True Stories of Over 100 Years...

(Chief Johnson and President George Bush)

(Chief Johnson with the Late Senator Strom Thurman
after Receiving the Strom Thurmond
Law Enforcement Award)

True Stories of Over 100 Years...

Strom Thurmond Awards
For
Excellence in Law Enforcement

Law Enforcement Coordinating Committee
Office of the U.S. Attorney

The Holiday Inn - Coliseum @ USC
Columbia, SC

April 13, 2001

True Stories of Over 100 Years…

35 WILLIE JOHNSON*
Greenville City Police Department

As police chief, Johnson has made a career out of serving and protecting our community. But he doesn't stop there. He also serves on the board for the Urban League and on the Board of Regents for Leadership Greenville, of which Johnson is a graduate.

True Stories of Over 100 Years…

BOB JONES *University*

GREENVILLE • SOUTH CAROLINA 29614-0001 • 864-242-5100 • ADMISSIONS 1-800-BJ-AND-ME

EXECUTIVE OFFICES
FAX 864-233-9829

March 1, 2007

Mr. Willie Johnson
Greenville City Police Chief
4 McGee Street, Suite 201C
Greenville, SC 29601

Dear Chief Johnson:

A while back when I picked up the morning newspaper, I learned of your impending retirement. My heart was sad. Your leadership of the police department has been good for Greenville—you have set a high standard of integrity. I've bragged about Greenville's quality of law enforcement in many places across the country where I've traveled. Thank you for your willingness to shoulder the burden, to take the heat, to do right.

All of us who live in the city are beneficiaries of your leadership. Our homes and institutions are safer. We all live in a complex age. Men call evil good and good evil. The lawbreaker is often justified, while the law enforcer is condemned. I have great respect for lawmen today who take their role seriously and refuse to be corrupted. I surely would hate to live in a city where the law enforcer joined complicity with the lawbreaker for the sake of gain.

Those of us who love this community and love the Lord will pray for the appointment of a worthy successor to follow in the noble tradition you have followed from your predecessors. Thank you for being a faithful man!

Kind regards,

Sincerely yours,

Bob Jones III

Bob Jones III
Chancellor

BJIII:ljn

(Letter of Commendation from Dr. Bob Jones, III)

True Stories of Over 100 Years...

UNITED STATES COURT OF APPEALS
For The Fourth Circuit
1100 East Main Street
Richmond, Virginia 23219

William W. Wilkins
  Chief Judge
H. Emory Widener, Jr.
J. Harvie Wilkinson III
Paul V. Niemeyer
Clyde H. Hamilton
Karen J. Williams

M. Blane Michael
Diana Gribbon Motz
William B. Traxler, Jr.
Robert B. King
Roger L. Gregory
Dennis W. Shedd
Allyson K. Duncan

March 2, 2007

Chief Willie L. Johnson
4 McGee Street
Greenville, SC 29601

Dear Chief Johnson:

    Today we join with your friends and colleagues in thanking you for thirty-seven years of outstanding work as a law enforcement officer for the City of Greenville. Both of us had the privilege of working with you while we each served as Solicitor, and we know firsthand of the exemplary work you did. With the pleasure one gets from seeing a good friend succeed, we've watched you earn your way from a patrolman working a beat to the highest rank in the Department.

    Your work has simply been outstanding, it has been recognized as such, and it has been appreciated by a grateful city. Best of luck as you retire. We will miss you.

Sincerely,

William W. Wilkins

William B. Traxler, Jr.

**(Letter of Appreciation from Federal Judges
William W. Wilkins and William B. Traxler, Jr.)**

(Chief Johnson Receives JHM Cooperation Award for
$101,000 for the Harold C. Jennings Foundation)

True Stories of Over 100 Years...

THE WHITE HOUSE

WASHINGTON

April 22, 2002

Mr. William Johnson
Chief of Police
Greenville Police Department
4 McGee Street
Greenville, South Carolina 29601-2207

Dear Willie:

Thank you for your assistance during my visit to Greenville, South Carolina.

I appreciate your efforts to help make my trip a success. I am grateful for your hard work and support.

Best wishes.

Sincerely,

George W. Bush

(Letter of Appreciation from President George W. Bush)

True Stories of Over 100 Years...

**(US Commemorative Postal Stamp Issued in
Honor of Chief Willie Johnson)**

True Stories of Over 100 Years...

115 Wren Way
Greenville, SC 29605
March 8, 2007

Chief Willie Johnson
Greenville Police Department
4 McGee Street
Greenville, SC 29601

Dear Chief Johnson,

I am very sorry that I will be unable to attend Law Enforcement Day at Macedonia Missionary Church on March 18th and your reception at Carolina First Center March 20th. Gladys and I are leaving for South America March 10th and will be gone for three weeks.

However, I want to wish you a long, happy retirement and good health. You have been dedicated and loyal to the Greenville Police Department and the City of Greenville and will be greatly missed.

I was so pleased to have you serve under my command and was impressed with your character and ability from the very beginning of your law enforcement career. You knew every aspect of the Greenville Police Department and you excelled in each position you held. I was especially pleased when the City recognized this and named you as our police chief.

Now, as you enter retirement, my wish is that you, Jannie and your family will enjoy it to the fullest. Thank you for a job well done.

Sincerely,

Harold C. Jennings

Harold C. Jennings
Chief of Police (Retired)
Greenville Police Department

(Congratulatory Letter from Chief Harold C. Jennings)

True Stories of Over 100 Years…

True Stories of Over 100 Years…

Captain Kelley's
Photos and Memorabilia

True Stories of Over 100 Years…

True Stories of Over 100 Years…

(My Father – Herbert Lee Kelley)

**(Calvin Kelley and Detective Bill Hitchins
Responding to an Armed Robbery)**

True Stories of Over 100 Years...

**(1970 Greenville City Police Department
Officer Waters and Calvin Kelley)**

True Stories of Over 100 Years…

(January 31, 1975 – Funeral of Lt. Frank Looper, Jr. and his father Frank Looper, Sr. shot and killed while investigating a suspicious person in his father's garage.)

True Stories of Over 100 Years…

(Greenville County Sheriff's Office 1980's Drug Bust)

True Stories of Over 100 Years...

**(Calvin Kelley pictured with Greenville County
Sheriff's Office Unmarked Cruiser)**

True Stories of Over 100 Years...

(Mrs. Helen – My Cub Scout Den Mother and the Mother of Rev. Jessie L. Jackson, Sr.)

True Stories of Over 100 Years…

(Retirement Plaque – 29 Years of Service)

True Stories of Over 100 Years...

(Grandchildren and Great Grandchild)

True Stories of Over 100 Years…

4-10-73

Greenville Council Votes To Reopen Chapman Road

Whites Arrested For Drugs In Black Community

Five Men Arraigned In Peoples Robbery

INSIDE THIS WEEK

Police search for man who escaped drug raid

Heroin Seized In City

Police Praised In Letter

(*Greenville News* Articles from Captain Kelley's Career)

True Stories of Over 100 Years…

Heroin Violation Is Charged

A 33-year-old Greenville man, free on bond on a charge of distributing heroin, was arrested Friday night and charged with possession with intent to distribute heroin and cocaine.

Dennis Vaughn of 16 Oak Creek Apartments, was arrested after sheriff's detectives and city police executed a search warrant for his apartment and seized a quantity of heroin and cocaine valued at $5,600, authorities said.

Vaughn was being held without bail late Friday.

City Police Hold 2 County Youths

A 17-year-old Taylors youth was arrested and a 16-year-old Slater girl was referred to juvenile authorities after they were accused of possessing marijuana.

Donald Montgomery of 115 Avon Drive, Taylors, was charged by Detective W. C. Butler of the City Police Department in a warrant issued by Magistrate Harry Dearmas.

City Patrolmen B. H. Brown and Calvin Kelly found a small quantity of marijuana in the couple's car on Woodland Way Circle in Cleveland park. The patrolmen said they stopped to investigate when they saw Montgomery rolling a cigarette in his parked car about 8 p.m. Tuesday.

Man Charged, 2 Teens Referred In 'Umbrella' Holdup At Grocery

AL DOZIER

Two teenagers today were referred to juvenile authorities and an adult charged in last night's armed robbery at the Seven-Eleven Store on Cleveland Street.

Bobby Lewis Irby, 21, of 32 Caine St. was charged by City Detective D. M. Bridges before Magistrate Claude McKinney. A 15-year-old and a 16-year-old were referred to Family Court.

Police said an umbrella was apparently carried under a coat to resemble a gun when assistant manager Lemuel Silver was confronted by two persons at the cash register.

Silver told police the bandit walked up to the counter with something poking out of his coat, but said nothing. Silver asked if it was a gun and the bandit nodded his head, and forced Silver to step away from the cash register.

The pair emptied the cash register of $50 and left in a car waiting outside. The car, witnesses said, was marked on the fender with the words, "soul sister."

The car was spotted a short time later on Washington Street by Patrolman Calvin Kelly. Irby was in the car and was arrested. The teenagers were later arrested at their home.

Police were still investigating a second armed robbery which occurred shortly after 11 p.m. Thursday at the Minit Saver Food Store, 706 N. Main St.

Approximately $20 was reported stolen when a lone bandit armed with a pistol held up Mrs. Ruth Morez. He reportedly left the scene in a car.

The bandit was described as wearing a black knit hat, a brown coat and in his 20s.

(*Greenville News* Articles from Captain Kelley's Career)

True Stories of Over 100 Years…

True Stories of Over 100 Years…

Captain Harper
Friends for Life

True Stories of Over 100 Years…

True Stories of Over 100 Years...

The two other authors of this book, Willie Johnson, and Calvin Kelley, Sr., are longtime friends and colleagues. Johnson is also from Laurens, and in the seventies, we were detective partners. I quickly learned Johnson was much more political than me. He was destined to become police chief or a politician. I must say I'm surprised by his retirement and that he hasn't thrown his hat in the ring for a political office. He attempted to teach me the importance of being political. One of Chief Jennings' pastimes was deer hunting, and so at the time, it became a pastime for others in the office. For me, I could not fathom getting up at three or four AM on a cold morning to sit in a tree and wait for a deer to appear. Chief Bridges' pastime was golf. Johnson talked me into playing golf with him and the chief. However, for me, that activity did not last either. Johnson became my boss when he became Chief of Police.

Kelley was once my counterpart when he was the Commander of Internal Affairs with the Greenville County Sheriff's Office. Kelley is a hand tool person. I think he's had every tool ever made. He and I traveled to Boston for NIAIA training (National Internal Affairs Investigator Association). It was both our first time in Boston. During our downtime, I wanted to explore the city. Kelley only wanted to visit all the tool shops. He won. I don't remember how many tool retailers we visited, but what little I know today about tools, Kelley gets the credit.

Kelley and I now live in the same neighborhood on the same street. This is the story about how I met Kelley, although he will not own it. When I was a young rookie officer, walking my beat on Main Street in

Greenville, I was on a one-way side street, E. North Street, to be exact. There was an instant downpour. I was getting soaked. Kelley was a detective. Kelley and his partner drove past me, slowed down, and asked if I wanted to get out of the rain. I said, "Yes." I ran to their car, and just as I reached for the rear door handle, they sped off. I could hear their laughter. They returned and said, "Okay, officer, we're joking. Get in." I reached for the door, and they sped off again, laughing harder than ever while I was getting soaked. I remember this like it was yesterday. True story. I think you'll agree; I must be a forgiving person.

True Stories of Over 100 Years…

True Stories of Over 100 Years…

Captain Kelley's
Acknowledgments

True Stories of Over 100 Years…

True Stories of Over 100 Years...

It is deeper than the thin blue line. On my journey, God has blessed me to cross paths with many influential people in my law enforcement career. Never would I have thought I would forge lifelong bonds that go beyond the thin blue line with three particular individuals. We share so many commonalities. We are all from humble beginnings and sought a better life in the midst of segregation. Our military background, along with our upbringing, is the basis for the discipline we have shown throughout our paths. Through our bond in law enforcement, we have shared highs and lows not only in our careers, but in our family lives. Chief Willie Johnson, Captain Willie Harper, and Sergeant Harold Beeks, I thank you for your friendship and your brotherhood. There are qualities in each of you that I recognized early on and did my best to emulate. From the professionalism to the way we took special pride in our appearance, we represented well.

Special recognition to the "Gentle Giant," Sgt. Harold Beeks, thank you. When I mentioned to you that I was thinking about working for the police department, you said, "Let me know how it goes." Once I was hired, I knew you would be perfect for the job. We were fortunate to become partners for a short while, and we became known as "Mutt and Jeff" due to the obvious size difference. I knew you had my back on and off the job. Your compassion for people was something I always admired about you. You went above and beyond with those you came in contact with, and that has stuck with me. May you continue to rest in peace. Semper Fi, or "always faithful."

Last but not least, thank you to my family for your unwavering support through the years.

True Stories of Over 100 Years…

Afterword

In summary, we, the three authors of this book, dedicated our lives serving, protecting, and caring for the Upstate Community of South Carolina. What began as jobs turned into successful careers in which we were fully vested. We continue to be passionate about the profession, and we hope that sharing our experiences has helped the general public understand the challenges law enforcement officers, especially those of color, endure behind the scenes. We salute those who have served, support those currently in office who operate with integrity, and extend well wishes to those who choose to serve in the future. Law enforcement officers must rebuild community trust in the profession. We must use our voices to account for more equity and accountability. As our world changes, may you be empowered to lead and serve with an abundance of grit and tenacity.

Retired Chief Willie Johnson
Retired Captain Calvin Kelley
Retired Captain Willie Harper

True Stories of Over 100 Years…

True Stories of Over 100 Years…

About the Authors

Retired Chief Willie Johnson

Retired Greenville, South Carolina Police Chief Willie Johnson served for 37 years in law enforcement and three years in the United States Army during the Vietnam War. While serving in the military, he was decorated with the Bronze Star Medal, South Vietnam Campaign Ribbon, and Combat Assault Award. Johnson was the first African American in the following positions: lieutenant, captain, department major and chief of police. As the 23rd Chief of Police, he raised the bar when he became the first chief to hold a college degree, which he received from Southern Wesleyan University in Central, South Carolina. He is married to his high school sweetheart, Jannie Ferguson Johnson, and they have two children. They reside in Greenville County, South Carolina. Johnson recognizes that education is the key to success and technology helps law enforcement lean into the fight to make and keep communities safer.

True Stories of Over 100 Years...

Retired Captain Calvin Kelley

Born the third child of six in Greenville, South Carolina to Herbert Lee and Ruby Mae Kelley during the years of segregation, Calvin Kelley was faced with disadvantages as well as advantages. Growing up in the South, serving his country as a marine and being a public servant to his community as a law enforcement officer for 29 years, Kelley realizes those are the experiences that have shaped him and what he believes as a man, a husband, a father, and as a law enforcement officer.

Although his parents expected great things from Kelley and his siblings, society had other views. There have been individuals, such as teachers from Sterling High School and organizations, such as Palmetto State Law Enforcement Officers Association (P.S.L.E.O.A.) that have encouraged and supported him and others like him, and for that, he is grateful.

True Stories of Over 100 Years...

Retired Captain Willie Harper

Willie Harper grew up in the city of Laurens, SC in the 1950s and sixties. Immediately after graduating from Sanders High School, he volunteered for the United States Army. After serving honorably for three years, he returned to his hometown for a few years before joining the Greenville Police Department in Greenville, SC. There, he served for 33 years and has been retired for 15 years. Since retirement, Harper's focus has been outdoor and fine art photography. A member of Reedy River Missionary Baptist Church in Mauldin, SC, Harper is a born-again Christian. He is married to his high school sweetheart, Winnie, and they have two children and three grandchildren. They currently reside in Greenville County, SC.

True Stories of Over 100 Years...

Contacting the Authors

Johnson can be contacted at
johnsow01@bellsouth.net

Kelley can be contacted at
gman6015@bellsouth.net

Harper can be contacted at
harperandharper@bellsouth.net

True Stories of Over 100 Years…

Made in the USA
Columbia, SC
09 February 2023

a9d783c7-3fda-4f8b-b108-d79d830efdcaR01